The Royal Naval Reviews
1935-1977

1
Lying peacefully at anchor at Spithead on the day before King George V reviewed his fleet in 1935 were RESOLUTION (nearest the camera), with RODNEY (left), BARHAM (behind) and REVENGE (right).

The Royal Naval Reviews
1935-1977

P. RANSOME-WALLIS

LONDON

IAN ALLAN LTD

Bibliography
British Vessels Lost at Sea 1939-45: HMSO
British Warship Names: Manning and Walker
Cruiser: S. L. Poole
Jane's Fighting Ships: Various volumes
Marine News: World Ship Society
Official Programmes for the Reviews of 1935, 1937, 1953, 1977
The Portsmouth News, Souvenir Issue, NATO Review, 1969
The War at Sea, vols 1-4: S. W. Roskill
Warships of World War II: Lenton and Colledge

Books by the same Author
On Railways at Home and Abroad
Locomotives through the Lens
Men of the Footplate
On Engines in Britain and France
The Concise Encyclopaedia of World Railway Locomotives (Editor and Contributor)
British Railways Today
The Last Steam Locomotives of British Railways (4 editions)
The Last Steam Locomotives of Eastern Europe
Die Letzten Dampflokomotiven Osteuropas
The Last Steam Locomotives of Western Europe (2 editions)
Die Letzten Dampflokomotiven Westeuropas
Preserved Steam Locomotives of Western Europe (vols I and II)
Southern Album
The Snowdon Mountain Railway (3 editions)
The World's Smallest Public Railway (5 editions)
All About Photographing Trains
Famous Railway Photographers — P. Ransome-Wallis
The Big Four
Roaming The Southern Rails

Ships and The Sea
The Royal Navy (3 editions)
Train Ferries of Western Europe
Eisenbahn-Fahren in Westeuropas
North Atlantic Panorama 1900-1976
Merchant Ship Panorama

All photographs in this book have been taken by the Author

First published 1982

ISBN 0 7110 1166 4

Published by Ian Allan Ltd, Shepperton, Surrey; and printed by Ian Allan Printing Ltd at their works at Coombelands in Runnymede, England

Contents

Foreword

by
**Admiral Sir Henry Leach, GCB, ADC,
First Sea Lord**

When you read this well documented account of the Spithead Reviews I expect you will be struck by how much the Royal Navy has decreased in size over the years. This reflects largely the changes that have taken place in the world and the position of Great Britain in it: the emergence of the two super powers and the reduction in our world wide responsibilities as the British Empire has evolved into the independent nations of the Commonwealth. To some extent this diminution is more one of numbers than of power. In World War II there was nothing to compare with today's nuclear submarine armed with strategic ballistic missiles; and even the 14-inch guns of yesterday's battleships would barely match the punch of the missile system of a modern destroyer.

Although the Royal Navy is no longer permanently stationed world wide it is still vitally important for the country to have well trained, balanced and effective maritime forces and for these to be capable of deployment overseas whenever they may be required. We are an island race dependent on trade for its living, 95% of which moves by sea. Much of the food and essential raw materials necessary for our survival have to be imported. Our merchant Fleet is the fourth largest in the world and contributes £1,000 million a year to our balance of payments. It has 1,100 ships over 500 tons and on any one day there are over 600 merchant ships at sea.

The protection of these crucial interests is only one of a number of war roles for the Royal Navy. These include the strategic nuclear deterrent, the protection of re-inforcements and supplies across the Atlantic and the Channel, mine counter-measures to keep open our ports and seaways, support of the NATO Strike Fleet in the Eastern Atlantic and protection of our sea lines of communication.

Equally important are the Royal Navy's tasks in times of peace and tension for which the presence and flexibility of maritime power is ideally suited. The advantages of sea power have been well recognised by the Soviets who over the past 20 years have built up a huge force of modern ships, submarines and maritime aircraft which goes far beyond the need to defend their own relatively small coastline. These forces are deployed throughout the world, often well outside the NATO boundaries, seeking areas of weakness which can be exploited to extend the communist ideology and Soviet influence. The free world must be prepared to counter them wherever they operate and so deter the Soviets from achieving their expansionist ambitions. As the largest Navy in Europe the Royal Navy has a major part to play in this requirement.

Henry Leach

Preface

There is no finer spectacle than that provided by a naval review, a fact appreciated by the many thousands who travel from near and far 'to see the ships'. There is, however, a comparatively small number of people whose interest in the individual ships is more discerning and technical than is that in the majority of the spectators. For them, a 'Review of the Fleet' provides a unique opportunity to see, to study and to photograph the ships. At no other time are so many warships assembled at one place and visiting foreign warships provide an added interest. Usually there is also present a number of merchant ships, many with famous names, while fleet auxiliaries, pleasure ships, ferries and even tugs are busily engaged in servicing the warships and carrying the many thousands of sightseers 'round the fleet'.

Traditionally in Britain such events are presented with exceptional panache and showmanship and the Royal Navy excels on these occasions.

I am very fortunate to have been present at the last five Royal Naval Reviews at Spithead, 1935-1977. By making on each occasion several 'voyages' round the ships, mostly in privately hired boats, I have been able to study and to photograph in detail most of the ships present and to record some of the developments which have taken place during 42 years. Most of the 'voyages' have been made during the assembling of the fleets before the actual day of the Review. On 'The Day' there is much activity around the ships with yachts, launches and pleasure craft in profusion: all of which makes quiet study and good photography almost impossible.

In this book, I have presented a selection of my photographs of naval and of some other ships seen at the last five Reviews. An attempt has been made to provide some history and details of most of the ships illustrated. I have also included in the book the anchorage plan of each Review and lists of the warships present. I only regret space is not available to show all the ships at all the Reviews!

Introduction

The first record of a Royal Review of the British Navy is that of the year 1415 when King Henry V reviewed his ships before sailing to do battle in France and achieving victory at Agincourt the same year. From then until 1977 there have been 43 Royal Naval Reviews, nearly all of which have taken place at Spithead. This is a roadstead between the shores of Hampshire and the Isle of Wight which provides an ideal deep-water anchorage, well sheltered but with good access to the English Channel to the east and, through the Solent, to the west. In recent times three Reviews were held elsewhere: in July 1919 King George V reviewed his ships off Southend to celebrate the naval victories of World War 1; in 1965 H.M. the Queen reviewed some of her ships in the Clyde and, in 1969, reviewed the Western Fleet in Torbay.

Numerically the largest of all the Spithead Reviews was that held in May 1944 and which was completely unpublicised. On that occasion King George VI reviewed the invasion fleets before the D-Day invasion of France. Some 800 ships, albeit nearly all small landing craft and minesweepers, were present.

The reasons for the holding of Fleet Reviews have varied considerably through the ages. Originally the objects were (1) mobilisation of the Fleet for war and, (2) to demonstrate to potential enemies or to friends, the naval strength of the nation. Examples of the first were those of 1415 already noted: of 1853

when there was a serious threat of war with Russia and of 16 July 1914 in preparation for the First World War with Germany. In the second category may be cited the Reviews of 1700 (visit of Peter the Great), 1814 (two visitors — the Czar of Russia and the King of Prussia), 1844 (the King of France was the guest), 1889 (the visit of Kaiser Wilhelm II and Admiral von Tirpitz) and others of less importance.

In the 19th century Queen Victoria's Golden Jubilee was celebrated by the Navy with a Review on 28 July 1887 and her Diamond Jubilee by another Review in June 1897. Since then, Royal Jubilees and Coronations have all been celebrated in this manner. No fewer than 17 Royal Naval Reviews were held during the reign of Queen Victoria, the first in 1842, the last in 1899 this latter being the occasion of a visit of part of the German Fleet. The Queen, however, was too frail to attend as indeed she had been in 1897 on the occasion of her Diamond Jubilee Review. The Prince of Wales (later King Edward VII) acted as her deputy on both of these occasions.

Royal Naval Reviews have provided unique opportunities for both the well-informed and the non-informed to see the development of naval technology from the caravels and carracks of the 15th century to the nuclear-powered missile-firing cruisers of today. Some of the most interesting developments are summarised here.

The Review of 1814 carried out by the Prince Regent was the last at which only sailing ships were present. On the next such occasion, in 1842, a number of ships had both sail and steam power. This was the first of Queen Victoria's Reviews and she sailed in the ROYAL GEORGE a 350-ton sailing ship which was very slow and gave Her Majesty much displeasure thereby. As a result, in 1843, the first steam-driven Royal Yacht was completed. Named VICTORIA AND ALBERT she was a paddle ship of 1,034 tons displacement, with a speed of $11\frac{1}{2}$ knots, wood-built but with a bell-mouthed brass funnel and two masts. Her name was changed to OSBORNE in 1855 when the second and much larger VICTORIA AND ALBERT (2,470 tons) was put into service.

In 1845 there was a Review of the 'Experimental Squadron' which consisted of ships by various designers to determine the fastest and most seaworthy among them. There was one steam warship and the Queen travelled in the steam paddle ship VICTORIA AND ALBERT.

In 1853 there was the first Naval Review at which most of the vessels present were steamships, both paddle and screw-driven.

The Review of 17 July 1867 was the first at which HM ships flew the White Ensign, and at that of 23 July 1887 a submarine was present for the first time. At both these Reviews the second VICTORIA AND ALBERT of 1855 carried the Royal Party.

In the Diamond Jubilee Review of 1897, the Prince of Wales reviewed the Fleet and the occasion was made noteworthy by Charles Parsons' turbine-driven vessel TURBINIA which steamed through the lines at unprecedented speeds, presaging the steam turbine-driven ships of the future.

Battle-cruisers appeared for the first time in July 1909 when King Edward VII reviewed the Fleet from the Royal Yacht VICTORIA AND ALBERT, built in 1899 and the third to carry the name. In July 1912 King George V saw the first naval aircraft take off from HMS LONDON.

At the Mobilisation Review of 16 July 1914, there was the greatest concentration of battleships ever seen and King George V, in VICTORIA AND ALBERT saw no fewer than 59 of these great ships. Ten years later, in July 1924, the same Monarch in the same ship, saw the first aircraft carrier assembled for review with other ships of the Fleet.

The Review to celebrate the Silver Jubilee of King George V took place in 1935. The latest of the Navy's big ships — the Battleships RODNEY and NELSON were of most interest though they were each by then eight years' old.

The Coronation Review of King George VI in May 1937 was noteworthy for the presence of three great visiting warships: ADMIRAL GRAF SPEE of Germany, the great French Battleship DUNKERQUE and the powerful, rebuilt Japanese Cruiser ASIGARA all of which became prominent in the history of the Second World War. On this occasion also, five British aircraft carriers were present.

In June 1953, to mark the occasion of the Coronation of Queen Elizabeth II, a large array of ships assembled at Spithead. This was the first review to be held after the end of the Second World War in 1945 and many of the ships present had fought in that war. The Review was also noteworthy in that only one Battleship, VANGUARD, was present and this was to be the last appearance at any Review of one of these great ships. Nine aircraft carriers were assembled and there was a large number of frigates and other anti-submarine ships which had played such a distinguished part in the defeat of the U-boat. On this occasion the Queen sailed in HMS SURPRISE to carry out the Review. VICTORIA AND ALBERT had been withdrawn and BRITANNIA was not completed.

In 1969 the Queen reviewed some of the ships of the North Atlantic Treaty Organisation (NATO) at Spithead. This was mainly a Review of smaller ships, mostly frigates and the British ships were greatly outnumbered by those of the other countries. It was noteworthy as being the first time ships equipped with guided missiles had been assembled at Spithead. On this occasion the Queen sailed in the Royal Yacht BRITANNIA, this being the first time this ship had carried the Royal Party at a Review.

The most recent Review was held to commemorate the Silver Jubilee of Queen Elizabeth II and took place at Spithead in June 1977. Again this was largely a Review of smaller ships most of which were equipped with missiles, a number of which had gas turbine propulsion and a few had nuclear power plants. The famous aircraft carrier ARK ROYAL was present for the first and only time at a Naval Review. On all these royal occasions the excellent service discipline and panache of the Royal Navy was apparent. We may have to wait a very long time before the ships again 'assemble at Spithead'.

Acknowledgements

In the preparation of this book I have been greatly encouraged and helped by the undermentioned gentlemen to whom my sincere thanks are due.

Captain R. Hart, CBE, DSO, DSC, RN	*Navy International*
Captain J. E. Moore, RN	Editor, *Jane's Fighting Ships*
Commander N. D. Cooper, RN	Ministry of Defence
Commander F. E. R. Phillips, RN	Ministry of Defence
Lt Commander J. P. Briggs, RN	HMS NELSON, Portsmouth
J. D. Brown Esq	Naval Historical Branch, Ministry of Defence
G. A. Osbon Esq	Late of National Maritime Museum
Frank S. White Esq	Ministry of Defence
Robert Avery Esq and M. Scott-Scott Esq	Britannia Royal Naval College, for reading and correcting the proofs

Abbreviations

As a reader and as an author I dislike abbreviations and it was my intention to do without them in the present book. However, without their use the text became over-burdened with long words and descriptions became cumbersome.

The present lists of abbreviations will be found to cover all those referring to types of naval ships as well as those in common use to describe technical terms. While the lists appear rather formidable, many of their entries are so well-known that frequent reference to them will be unnecessary.

The descriptions of naval ships have changed considerably over the last 50 years. For example, what in 1935 was a 'sloop' became an 'escort vessel' in 1937 and a 'frigate' in 1953, thus requiring three abbreviations for the same type of ship! In passing, what a pity the term 'Corvette' never appeared in any of the reviews described. They did such essential and gallant work during WW2.

Ship Abbreviations

A/C	AIRCRAFT CARRIER
A/D/V	AIRCRAFT DIRECTION VESSEL
ARM/SHIP	ARMOURED SHIP
B/C	BATTLE CRUISER
B/S	BATTLESHIP
BV	BOOM VESSEL
C	CRUISER
CS	COASTAL SURVEY
CSH	COASTAL SURVEY HYDROGRAPHY
D	DESTROYER
D.C.	DARING CLASS
DDR	RADAR PICKET DESTROYER
D/S	DIVING SHIP
D/T	DIVING SHIP TENDER
E	ESCORT
E/D	ESCORT DESTROYER
F	FRIGATE
F/B	FERRYBOAT
F/L	FLOTILLA LEADER
F.P.V.	FISHERY PROTECTION VESSEL
F S/M	FLEET SUBMARINE
F/T	FLEET TENDER
FTB	FAST TRAINING BOAT
H/C	HELICOPTER CRUISER
H.S.	HOSPITAL SHIP
IS/V	INSHORE TRAINING VESSEL
L/C	LIGHT CRUISER
LCT	LANDING CRAFT TANKS
LSH	LANDING SHIP HEADQUARTERS
MCM	MINE COUNTER MEASURE
M/H (FP)	MINE HUNTER (FISHERY PROTECTION)
M/LR	MINE LAYER
M/S (O)	MINESWEEPER (OCEAN)
N.L.	NET LAYER
O.T.	OIL TANKER
P	PATROL VESSEL
P S/M	PATROL SUBMARINE
RFA	ROYAL FLEET AUXILIARY
RMAS	ROYAL MARITIME AUXILIARY SERVICE
RNAS	ROYAL NAVAL AUXILIARY SERVICE
RNR	ROYAL NAVAL RESERVE
R/S	HEAVY REPAIR SHIP
S	SLOOP
S/M	SUBMARINE
S.M.D.S.	SUBMARINE DEPOT SHIP
S/M SSN	NUCLEAR POWERED ATTACK SUBMARINE
S/S	SURVEY SHIP
SUP.	SUPPORT SHIP
Tr.S.	TRAINING SHIP
T/S RMA	TRIAL SHIP, ROYAL MARITIME AUXILIARY SERVICE
VSTOL/C	HELICOPTER VERTICAL SHORT LANDING AND TAKE OFF CARRIER

Technical Abbreviations

AA	Anti-aircraft
A, B, C, X and Y	Gun turret positions
A/S	Anti-submarine
ASROC	Anti-submarine rocket
ASW	Anti-submarine weapons
ATW	Ahead thrown weapons
bhp	Brake horsepower
CAAIS	Computer assisted action information system
C-in-C	Commander in Chief
cpp	Controllable Pitch Propeller
DASH	Drone Anti-Submarine Helicopter
FBM	Fleet Ballistic Missile
FRAM I and II	Fleet Rehabilitation and Modernisation I and II
HA/LA	High Angle/Low Angle
HMS	Her (His) Majesty's Ship
ihp	Indicated horsepower
mm	Millimetre
MV	Motor Vessel
NTDS	Naval Tactical Data System
PS	Paddle steamer
psi	Pounds per Square Inch
RAN	Royal Australian Navy
RCN	Royal Canadian Navy
RHN	Royal Hellenic Navy
RIN	Royal Indian Navy
RN	Royal Navy
RNZN	Royal New Zealand Navy
RPN	Royal Pakistan Navy
shp	Shaft Horsepower
SLCM	Submarine Launched Cruise Missile
SPV	Self-propelled Vehicle
SS	Steamship
tD	Tons Displacement
tG	Tons Gross
VDS	Variable Depth Sonar
WT	Water tube
WW1	World War One (First World War)
WW2	World War Two (Second World War)

NB: Displacement tonnage (tD) is often given thus eg 10,000/12,000 tD. The first figures represent the Standard Displacement; the second figure is the Full Load Displacement. Where only one figure is quoted this is the Standard Displacement.

Figures in parenthesis after the *Completion* date refer to (overall length × maximum breadth × mean draught) all in feet.

Silver Jubilee Review 1935

The Royal Naval Review at Spithead on 16 July 1935 was in celebration of the Silver Jubilee of King George V who ascended to the throne in 1910. King George entered the Navy in 1877 at the age of 12 years and remained a serving officer until the death of his elder brother, Edward, opened to him the eventual accession to the throne. At this time he was 27 years of age and had achieved the rank of Commander. He was then in command of HMS CRESCENT, a first-class Cruiser and his fourth command.

There were 157 naval ships of all types present at the Review, the most modern being the four 'Leander' class 7,000-ton 6-inch cruisers completed in 1933-1934. On this occasion, no foreign warships were present. The King, with Queen Mary, carried out the Review from the Royal Yacht VICTORIA AND ALBERT in which they had embarked the previous day.

The Review commenced at 1400 hours with the reception by the King of the Board of Admiralty and his Flag Officers on board VICTORIA AND ALBERT. At 1600 hours the Royal Yacht entered the lines and proceeded between lines D and E (see plan) returning to anchor at the head of the lines by passing between lines F and G. All ships were dressed overall with their companies manning ship and each gave 'three cheers' as the Yacht passed slowly by. At 1800 hours, the Review area was opened to the public, at 2200 the ships were illuminated and the area cleared. At midnight the illumination ceased.

On the following morning at 0800 hours the Royal Yacht led the Fleet to sea for exercises before returning to berth at Portsmouth at 1440.

The sixth Royal Naval Review of the 20th century was over.

2

2
VICTORIA AND ALBERT Royal Yacht. *Completed:* 1899 (439¼×40×18) 4,700 tD. A steel ship sheathed with wood and coppered. *Complement:* 363 officers and men including a Royal Marine Band. Commanded by a Rear Admiral. *Armament:* Two 6-pdr bronze saluting guns. *Propulsion:* Twin screws driven by two sets of vertical triple expansion engines: 11,800 ihp: 20 knots. She carried the Royal Party at both the 1935 and the 1937 Reviews and, despite a reputation (said to be unjustified) as a 'tender' ship, she was well-loved by both King Edward VII and King George V. During the Second World War she was used as an accommodation ship at Portsmouth and was scrapped in 1954. VICTORIA AND ALBERT was the third Royal Yacht to carry the name. The first was a small paddle steamer with one funnel and two masts, built for Queen Victoria in 1843. Her name was changed to *Osborne* in 1855 and she was broken up in 1868. The second VICTORIA AND ALBERT was completed in 1855 and was also a wood-built paddle steamer with two funnels and three masts. She was not unlike her successor in appearance and was a great favourite with Queen Victoria. She was broken up in 1904.

1935

HM Ship	Type	HM Ship	Type	HM Ship	Type	HM Ship	Type
ACASTA	D	DUNDALK	M	KEMPENFELT	F/L	SCIMITAR	D
ACHERON	D	DUNOON	M	KINGFISHER	S	SCOTSMAN	D
ACHILLES	C	ECHO	D	LEANDER	C	SCOUT	D
ACTIVE	D	ECLIPSE	D	LONDON	C	SEAHORSE	S/M
ALBURY	M/S	EFFINGHAM	C	LUCIA	S.M.D.S.	SEA LION	S/M
ALRESFORD	M/S	ELECTRA	D	LYDD	M/S	SEARCHER	D
AMAZON	D	ELGIN	M	L 21	S/M	SELKIRK	M/S
AMBUSCADE	D	ENCOUNTER	D	L 26	S/M	SEVERN	S/M
ANTELOPE	D	ESCAPADE	D	L 27	S/M	SHARK	S/M
ANTHONY	D	ESCORT	D	L 54	S/M	SHROPSHIRE	C
ARDENT	D	ESK	D	L 69	S/M	SKATE	D
ARROW	D	EXMOUTH	F/L	L 71	S/M	SKIPJACK	S
AUSTRALIA	C	EXPRESS	D	MACKAY	F/L	SNAPPER	S/M
BARHAM	B/S	FAME	D	MAINE	H.S.	STARFISH	S/M
BASILISK	D	FAULKNOR	F/L	MONTROSE	F/L	STRONGHOLD	D
BEAGLE	D	FEARLESS	D	NELSON	B/S	STURDY	D
BLANCHE	D	FERMOY	M/S	NEPTUNE	C	STURGEON	S/M
BOADICEA	D	FIREDRAKE	D	NIMBLE	F/B	SUTTON	M
BOREAS	D	FLINDERS	S/S	ORION	C	SWORDFISH	S/M
BRAZEN	D	FORESIGHT	D	OTWAY	S/M	TEDWORTH	M
BRILLIANT	D	FORESTER	D	OXLEY	S/M	TEMPEST	D
BROKE	F/L	FORTUNE	D	PANGBOURNE	M/S	TENEDOS	D
BULLDOG	D	FOXHOUND	D	PEGASUS	A/C	THANET	D
CAIRO	C	FROBISHER	C	PORPOISE	S/M	THRUSTER	D
CALEDON	C	FURIOUS	A/C	QUEEN ELIZABETH	B/S	TITANIA	S.M.D.S.
CALYPSO	C	FURY	D	RAMILLIES	B/S	TIVERTON	M/S
CAMPBELL	F/L	GODETIA	F.P.V.	RENOWN	B/C	TORRID	D
CARDIFF	C	GUARDIAN	N.L.	RESOLUTION	B/S	VALIANT	D
CLYDE	S/M	HALCYON	S	RESTLESS	D	VALOROUS	D
CODRINGTON	F/L	HAREBELL	F.P.V.	REVENGE	B/S	VESPER	D
COMET	D	HARRIER	S	RODNEY	B/S	VINDICTIVE	C
COURAGEOUS	A/C	HAWKINS	C	ROWENA	D	VISCOUNT	D
COVENTRY	C	HOOD	B/C	ROYAL SOVEREIGN	B/S	VIVIEN	D
CRESCENT	D	HUSSAR	S	SABLE	D	WAKEFUL	D
CRUSADER	D	H.32	S/M	SABRE	D	WESSEX	D
CURACOA	C	H.44	S/M	SALADIN	D	WINCHELSEA	D
CYCLOPS	S.M.D.S.	H.50	S/M	SALMON	S/M	WINCHESTER	D
CYGNET	D	INDUS	S	SALTASH	M/S	WOOLSTON	D
DEVONSHIRE	C	IRON DUKE	T.S.	SALTBURN	M/S	WRESTLER	D
DOUGLAS	F/L	KEITH	F/L	SARDONYX	D		

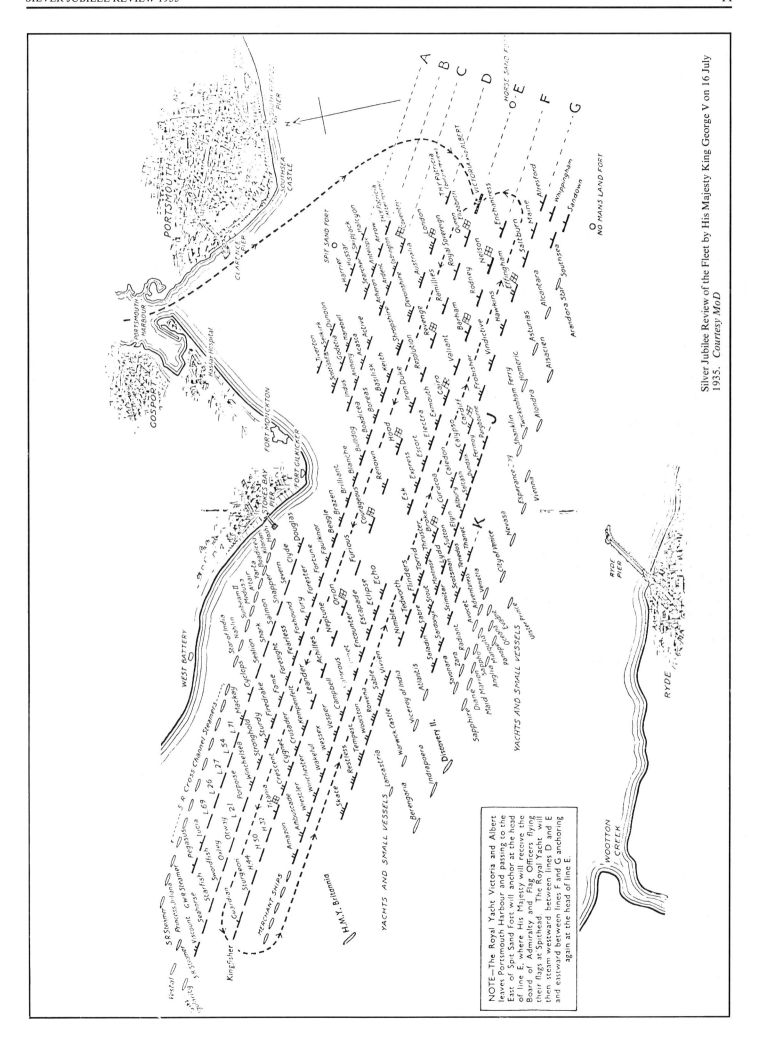

Silver Jubilee Review of the Fleet by His Majesty King George V on 16 July 1935. *Courtesy MoD*

3

4

3
QUEEN ELIZABETH B/S Fleet Flagship, Mediterranean Fleet, senior Flagship in the 1935 Review. She was completed in 1915 and was the first of the five ships of the class, being followed during the next year by WARSPITE, BARHAM, MALAYA and VALIANT in that order. Her technical description was the same as that given for VALIANT (Plate 4) except that she had Parsons direct drive turbines instead of those of Brown-Curtis design. During WWI she saw service in the Dardanelles as well as in the North Sea and during 1917-1919 was the Flagship of Earl Beatty. She was reconstructed with the rest of the class between 1925 and 1933, the most obvious alteration to her appearance being the trunking of her two funnels and the complete re-modelling of her bridge and fighting top. She retained her stern walk. In 1938, she began a further drastic reconstruction to her armour, an increase in her anti-aircraft armament and she was re-engined with single-reduction-geared turbines and new boilers. Her speed was 24 knots. She joined the Fleet at Scapa Flow at the end of 1940. She was in the Mediterranean Fleet in 1941 fighting at Crete and later in the war was sent to the East Indies. A pleasant story is told of her meeting the Cunard SS *Queen Elizabeth* in mid-Atlantic in 1943. HMS QUEEN ELIZABETH made a signal to her namesake which read 'Snap'! With many other great ships she was broken up in 1948.

4
VALIANT B/S Second Battle Squadron. Home Fleet. *Complement:* 1,150 officers and men. *Armament:* Eight 15-inch guns in twin turrets, 12 6-inch, four 4-inch AA and a number smaller guns. *Armour:* heavily armoured along both sides of the ship at level of water-line and above to a depth of 18 inches. Turrets and barbettes also well protected and the ship had anti-torpedo bulges along each side above and below the water line. *Completed:* 1916 ($639\frac{1}{4} \times 104 \times 33\frac{1}{2}$ max) 31,000/35,000 tD. *Propulsion:* Quadruple screws with Brown-Curtis direct drive high pressure turbines on the wing shafts and intermediate and low pressure turbines on the inner shafts. Cruising turbines geared to the wing shafts. 75,000 shp: 25 knots. Twenty-four oil fired boilers. VALIANT was one of five battleships of the *Queen Elizabeth* Class completed between 1913 and 1915 and which saw active service during WWI. With BARHAM she fought at Jutland. As built, the ships had two funnels. All five were extensively modernised during 1925 and 1933, their two funnels being trunked into one. In the years immediately before the outbreak of WWII four of the five ships, WARSPITE, VALIANT, MALAYA and QUEEN ELIZABETH were again completely refitted and their anti-aircraft armament increased. They were re-engined with single-reduction-geared turbines. Their appearance was again completely altered. Only BARHAM was not refitted owing to the outbreak of war. VALIANT was a valuable fighting ship and saw service during WWII off Norway in 1940, and in the many Mediterranean battles between 1940 and 1943. She ended the war in the Far East theatre of conflict. She was broken up in 1948.

5

6

5
REVENGE B/S Flagship of Second in Command, Mediterranean Fleet.
Completed: 1916 (624½ × 102½ × 28½) 29,150/33,500 tD. *Complement:*
Between 1,010 and 1,146 officers and men. *Armament:* Eight 15-inch in twin
turrets, 12 6-inch, five 4-inch AA and a number of smaller guns. Two 21-inch
torpedo tubes (submerged). *Armour:* 18-inch belt on each side protecting
machinery spaces and magazines. Lighter armour above and on turrets and
barbettes: anti-torpedo bulges. *Propulsion:* Quadruple screws driven by
Parsons direct drive turbines, with cruising turbines geared to wing shafts. 18
boilers — oil fired. 42,356 shp: 23 knots without, and 22 knots with, anti-
torpedo bulges. REVENGE was the first of five battleships which were smaller
and slower versions of the QUEEN ELIZABETH Class. She was four feet
longer overall than her sisters. She was the only one of the class present at
Jutland in 1916. All the ships were refitted twice between 1924 and 1937 but
no major reconstruction was undertaken. However, anti-aircraft armament
was increased. REVENGE spent much of her service during WWII on North
Atlantic convoy support duties. She was broken up in 1948

6
RESOLUTION B/S First Battle Squadron, Mediterranean Fleet. Details
as for REVENGE (Plate 5) but length overall 620½ feet. She could be
distinguished from other ships of the class by the addition of a clinker screen to
her funnel. Her active service in WWII was mainly in the North Atlantic and
in the Norwegian campaign. She was broken up in 1948.

7

8

7

ROYAL SOVEREIGN B/S First Battle Squadron, Mediterranean Fleet. *Completed:* 1916. Details and description as for REVENGE (Plate 5). She was the only ship of the class to retain her pole mainmast, all others being given tripod masts on refitting. During WWII she fought at Calabria in 1940 and spent much of the rest of the war as convoy support in the North Atlantic. In 1944 she was loaned to Russia, being re-named ARKHANGELSK. She was returned in 1949 and was scrapped.

8

RAMILLIES B/S First Battle Squadron, Mediterranean Fleet. *Completed* by Cammell Laird in 1917 after being part-built by Beardmore. Details and description as for REVENGE (Plate 5) but length overall was 620½ feet. She was the first ship to have anti-torpedo bulges and those were much deeper than those of other ships. She was refitted twice between the wars but, apart from an increase in her anti-aircraft armament, was not modernised. During WWII RAMILLIES was in action in the Mediterranean in 1940 and on convoy duties in the North Atlantic in 1941. In May 1942 with ILLUSTRIOUS, INDOMITABLE, HERMIONE and seven destroyers she assisted in the capture of Diego Saurez, Madagascar. During the operation she was torpedoed by a Japanese midget submarine launched from a larger parent submarine. She was repaired at Durban and later, in 1944, took part in the bombardment of the Normandy beaches. She was sold for scrapping in 1948.

9

RODNEY B/S Second Battle Squadron, Home Fleet. *Completed:* 1927 33,900/41,000 tD *Complement:* 1,361 officers and men. *Armament:* Nine 16-inch guns in triple turrets; 12 6-inch, six 4.7-inch AA and other smaller guns. Two 24.5-inch torpedo tubes. She later carried two aircraft and had a catapult on 'C' turret. *Armour:* Mainly concentrated in the forepart of the ship to protect magazines. *Propulsion:* Twin screws each driven by Curtis Brown single-reduction-geared turbines. 45,000 shp: 23 knots. Like her sister ship NELSON, she was a much reduced version of a 48,000-ton battle cruiser which was vetoed by the Washington Treaty of 1922. The revised design resulted in all the firepower of her main armament being placed forward of the bridge, engine rooms and boilers. RODNEY had a very busy time during WWII seeing action off Norway in 1940, Malta convoys 1941-2, North Africa 1942-3, Sicily and Salerno in 1943 and at the Normandy beaches in 1944. She also helped to sink the German battleship BISMARCK after a long chase in 1941. She was broken up in 1948.

10

NELSON B/S Flagship of C-in-C Home Fleet, the Earl of Cork and Orrery. *Completed:* 1927 (710×106×30 mean) 33,500/40,100 tD). Details as for RODNEY (Plate 9) but she carried only one seaplane lifted outboard and inboard by crane. NELSON served in both the Atlantic and Mediterranean during WWII. She was mined in Loch Ewe early on in the war and, in September 1941, was torpedoed while on convoy escort duty to Malta. She was at the invasion of Sicily, then off Salerno in 1943 and covered the Normandy landings in 1944. She was broken up in 1949. This photograph shows the large bridge structure which supported the fire control directors and contained sea-cabins as well as chartroom etc. The secondary armament of 6-inch guns in twin turrets can be clearly seen.

9

10

11

12

11
Immediately before leaving for the Review Anchorage, NELSON and HOOD were tied up alongside in Portsmouth Dockyard where they were photographed. The masts and spars of VICTORY, dressed overall, can be seen behind NELSON.

12
IRON DUKE (Gunnery Training Ship, former battleship) *Completed:* 1914 (614×89½×32) 21,250 tD. *Complement:* 583 officers and men. Armament: Six 13.5-inch and 12 6-inch guns (she was partly disarmed and most of her armour removed as a result of the London Treaty of 1931). *Propulsion:* Quadruple screw: Parsons direct drive turbines. Speed since 1932 reduced to 18 knots.   For the first two years of WWI she was the Flagship of Admiral Jellicoe and wore his flag at the Battle of Jutland. During WWII she was employed as a base ship and a coast defence ship at Scapa Flow. She was damaged by a near-miss from a German bomber in October 1939 and had to be beached. She maintained her duties thereafter, aground. She was broken up at Faslane in 1946.

13

14

13
HOOD B/C Flagship of the Battle Cruiser Squadron, Home Fleet.
Completed: 1920 (860×105¼×31½) 42,100/47,500 tD. Peacetime
complement was 1,477 officers and men. *Armament:* Eight 15-inch guns in
twin turrets; 12 5.5-inch and 27 smaller guns were her secondary armament.
Six 21-inch torpedo tubes. *Armour:* HOOD was strongly built and was
heavily armoured with a 12-inch main belt extending to her turrets.
Nonetheless, she was a very beautiful and well-proportioned ship and, for
many years, was the world's largest fighting ship. *Propulsion:* She had four
screws each driven by Brown-Curtis single-reduction-geared turbines
developing a total of 144,000 shp for a maximum speed of 32 knots. She had
24 oil-fired Yarrow boilers. Between the wars she made a number of prestige
visits to overseas countries and, for many foreigners, the 'mighty HOOD' was
the symbol of British naval power.

14
RENOWN B/C. *Completed:* 1916. (794×102⅔×27) 32,000/37,400 tD.
Complement: About 1,200 officers and men. *Armament:* Six 15-inch, twelve
4-inch, eight 4-inch AA and a number of smaller guns. 10 21-inch torpedo
tubes. Four aircraft with catapult. *Armour:* 9-inch belt amidships; 6-inch
armour for turrets; 1-inch deck armour. *Propulsion:* Quadruple screws driven
by Brown-Curtis direct drive turbines: 112,000 shp: 31 knots but was said
rarely to have achieved this speed in service. She was provided with
anti-torpedo bulges and had other alterations made during a long refit 1923-26.
Soon after being present at the Review she was again in dockyard hands until
1939 for major reconstruction which was more extensive than that of her sister
ship REPULSE (Plates 43 and 49). On this occasion she was re-engined with
single reduction geared turbines, developing 120,000 shp for 29 knots. Her
secondary armament was altered to 20 4.5-inch HA/LA and 20 smaller guns.
(During the early years of the war, twelve of her 4.5inch guns were replaced by
62 20mm AA). Her torpedo tubes were removed. She emerged with two
funnels of equal height. During WWII she was engaged in many patrols and
sorties in northern waters and she was in action against the German ships
GNEISENAU and SCHARNHORST during the Norwegian campaign, the
former ship being severely damaged. In August 1940 RENOWN replaced
HOOD as Admiral Somerville's Flagship in Force H based at Gibraltar and
she saw much action both in the Mediterranean and the Atlantic, taking part in
the hunt for the TIRPITZ. In 1944-45 she was attached to the Eastern Fleet
and then in the East Indies. She survived the war and was broken up in 1948.

15

16

15
FURIOUS A/C (786¼×89¾×21⅔) 22,450/24,700 tD. *Completed* in July 1917 as a heavy cruiser with two 18-inch guns in single turrets. Four months after completion the forward gun was removed (some accounts state it was never mounted) and was replaced by a flight deck. She had a large single funnel and a tripod mast. After a period in reserve after WWI she was completely reconstructed during 1921-25 with a flight deck covering nearly the whole length of the ship and with hangars below this deck. Her single large funnel was removed and her uptakes discharged right aft beneath the after end of the flight deck. She was a fast ship with a maximum speed in excess of 32 knots. She had quadruple screws powered by single-reduction-geared Brown-Curtis turbines developing 90,000 shp. FURIOUS was kept fully occupied during WWII and for a time was the only carrier with the Home Fleet. Her aircraft gave convoy cover. She took part in the battle for Norway, and she took fighters up to Narvik. She was then to be found transporting aircraft to Gibraltar and to Malta and again gave useful cover to fast troop convoys in the Atlantic. Her aircraft gave excellent cover to the Allied Forces in operation 'Torch' — the invasion of North Africa in October-November 1942. Soon after, she was again patrolling the Denmark Strait when the German TIRPITZ was thought to be trying to 'break out'. Her refit in August 1943 was badly needed but, soon after, she was hard at work until the end of the war. This gallant old ship was scrapped in 1948.

16
COURAGEOUS A/C Flagship of the Home Fleet Aircraft Carriers. *Completed:* 1917 as a heavily armed cruiser carrying four 15-inch and 16 4-inch guns. She had belts of 3-inch armour amidships (786¼×81¼× 22) 22,500/26,500 tD. *Propulsion:* Quadruple screws were driven by Parsons single-reduction-geared turbines developing 90,000 shp: 32 knots. In November 1917 she was in action against a German fleet at the Battle of Heligoland Bight. She was over-gunned and extravagant to run and, in 1924, was withdrawn to be completely rebuilt as an aircraft carrier. She re-entered service in 1928. Her heavy guns had been removed and replaced by 10 5.5-inch and six 4-inch AA. Later she was again re-armed with 16 4.7-inch HA/LA and 56 smaller guns. She was re-engined with four sets of single-reduction-geared turbines. She could accommodate 48 aircraft. COURAGEOUS had a brief and undistinguished career during WWII being sunk by torpedoes from a U-boat off the west coast of Ireland on 17 September 1939. Her sister ship was GLORIOUS (Plate 51)

17

SHROPSHIRE C First Cruiser Squadron, Mediterranean Fleet.
Completed: 1929 (633×66×17) 9,830 tD. *Complement:* 650 officers and
men. *Armament:* Eight 8-inch, four 4-inch AA and four 3-pounder guns.
Eight 21-inch torpedo tubes in quadruple mountings. One aircraft with
catapult. *Armour:* Main belt 3-inch; turrets 2-inch; deck 1½-inch.
Propulsion: Quadruple screw — Parsons single-reduction-geared turbines:
80,000 shp: 32¼ knots. Eight Admiralty 3-drum boilers. With their three tall
funnels and high freeboard, these 'County' Class cruisers came in for much
criticism as being always large and obvious targets. But, during WWII, they
proved to be most valuable ships and all had busy and usually successful
careers. SHROPSHIRE was engaged early in war in the South Atlantic trying
to intercept German surface raiders and later supported the East African
campaign in 1941. In 1943 she was transferred to the Royal Australian Navy
and saw action in the Far East and in the Pacific War, at times under
American command. She survived the war and was broken up in Scotland in
1955.

18

19

18
DEVONSHIRE C First Cruiser Squadron, Mediterranean Fleet.
Completed: 1929. One of the four 'London' Class cruisers and a sister ship to
SHROPSHIRE (Plate 17). Her dimensions and details are identical with that
ship. She also had a busy time during WWII. In 1940 she rescued the King of
Norway from Tromso and took part actively in the evacuation of troops from
Andalsnes. She then worked from Scapa with units of the Home Fleet in the
blockade of the Denmark Strait. She took part in the expedition to Dakar and
then was acting as cover for Russian convoys. In 1941 she sank the successful
German raider ATLANTIS in the South Atlantic. In 1942 she played an
active part in the capture of Diego Suarez in Madagascar. It is pleasant to
record that DEVONSHIRE was principal escort to NORFOLK in which
King Haakon of Norway and his family returned to Oslo after the German
defeat in 1945. She was broken up in 1954.

19
AUSTRALIA C First Cruiser Squadron, Mediterranean Fleet. *Completed:*
1928 (630×68¼×16¼) 9,870 tD. *Complement:* 679 officers and men.
Armament: Eight 8-inch, four 4-inch AA and 20 smaller guns. Eight 21-inch
torpedo tubes in quadruple mountings. One 'Osprey' flying boat with
catapult. *Armour:* Main belt 4-inch; deck 1½-inch; turrets 3-inch. *Propulsion:*
Quadruple screw — Brown Curtis single-reduction-geared turbines 80,000
shp: 31½ knots. With CANBERRA, she was one of the two 'Kent' Class
cruisers of the Royal Australian Navy and one of the first seven 'County'
Class cruisers. During WWII she took part in the attack on Dakar in 1940 and
afterwards worked for a time with the Home Fleet but, in 1941, she returned to
Australia and was then very actively engaged in the Pacific war until the end of
hostilities. She survived but not without considerable damage and casualties.
Her voyage, via New York, to Britain for a refit in 1945 was something of a
triumph for this very gallant ship. She was broken up at Barrow-in-Furness in
1955.

20

21

20
VINDICTIVE C Ninth Cruiser Squadron, Reserve Fleet. *Completed:* 1918. (605×58×19) 9,750 tD. *Armament:* Six 7.5-inch and nine smaller guns. Six 21-inch torpedo tubes. Carried one aircraft on a catapult replacing 'B' gun. *Armour:* 3-inch side armour. 1-inch deck armour. *Propulsion:* Quadruple screws driven by Parsons single-reduction-geared turbines: 60,000 shp: 30 knots. Eight Yarrow boilers. VINDICTIVE was one of four fast light cruisers, the other three not being completed until 1919-1924. She was originally named CAVENDISH but her name was changed when it was decided to complete her as an aircraft carrier. However, she was rebuilt as a cruiser during 1923-25, but had one less gun than the other three ships owing to her having an aircraft catapult. In 1936 she was converted to a training ship but fought as a cruiser during the early part of WWII when she assisted in the evacuation of British troops from Narvik in 1940. Later that year she was fitted out as a repair ship and spent most of the rest of the war at Freetown, Sierra Leone. She was broken up in 1946. NB: The photograph reproduced here was taken in 1932.

21
FROBISHER C Ninth Cruiser Squadron Reserve Fleet Cadet Training ship. *Completed:* 1924 (605×65×17½) 9,860 tD. *Complement:* About 715 officers and men. *Armament:* Nine 6-inch, three 4-inch AA and 16 smaller guns. Six 21-inch torpedo tubes. *Armour:* Main belt 3-inch; deck 1½-inch; lighter armour bow and stern. Anti-torpedo bulges. *Propulsion:* Quadruple screw: Parsons direct drive turbine with geared turbines for cruising. 65,000 shp: 30½ knots. In 1939 she was refitted and re-armed and served with the Eastern Fleet and later with the Home Fleet during WWII. In 1944 she was damaged by a torpedo from a U-boat while off the Normandy beaches where, with the help of a spotter plane, she was successfully destroying a number of German tanks at a range of 15,000 yards. A truly remarkable feat for an old ship and old guns! She returned to Portsmouth and, in 1945, again became a training ship. She was broken up in 1949.

22

23

22
CAIRO C. *Completed:* 1919 (450×43½×14¼) 4,200 tD. *Complement:* 437 officers and men. *Armament:* Five 6-inch, two 3-inch and 14 smaller guns. Eight 21-inch torpedo tubes in four twin mountings. *Armour:* 3-inch side armour and lighter protection elsewhere. *Propulsion:* Twin screws driven by Parsons single-reduction-geared turbines developing 40,000shp for 29 knots.   CAIRO was one of the last five 'C' ('Carlisle') Class cruisers to be built. These ships could be recognised from the earlier 'C's by their having a 'trawler bow' with pronounced hard chine. The earlier ships were very wet forward in even a moderate sea. In 1939 CAIRO and three other 'Carlisle' Class cruisers were converted to anti-aircraft ships and their armament then consisted of eight 4-inch AA guns, a multiple pompom and some smaller guns. Three of the earlier 'C' Class were previously converted. (Plate 53). During WWII, CAIRO was on escort duties for minelayers and then for Norwegian convoys. She was bombed and damaged during the evacuation from Narvik in May, 1940. Later, she served in the Mediterranean and while forming part of the escort of a Malta convoy in August 1942, was torpedoed by an Italian submarine. She was so badly damaged that she had to be sunk by our own forces.

23
COVENTRY C First Cruiser Squadron, Mediterranean Fleet. *Completed:* 1918 (450×43½×14½) 4,290 tD. *Complement:* 400 officers and men. *Armament:* Five 6-inch, two 3-inch AA and 14 smaller guns. Eight 21-inch torpedo tubes. *Propulsion:* Twin screws: Brown-Curtis single-reduction-geared turbines: 40,000 shp: 29 knots.   The five ships of the 'Ceres' Class were very wet forward even in a moderate sea and later ships of the 'Carlisle' Class (Plate 22) were provided with trawler bows. COVENTRY (whose original name was CORSAIR) with her sister ship CURLEW was converted to an anti-aircraft ship in 1935-36 and later all five of the later 'C' (or 'Carlisle') Class were so converted.

24

LEANDER C. *Completed:* 1935. ($554\frac{1}{2} \times 55\frac{1}{4} \times 16$) 7,140/9,500 t.D. *Complement:* 550 officers and men. *Armament:* Eight 6-inch, four 4-inch and 19 smaller guns. Eight 21-inch torpedo tubes in quadruple mountings. One aircraft on catapult abaft the funnel. *Armour:* 4-inch side armour amidships; 1-inch turrets and bridge; 2-inch deck armour. *Propulsion:* Quadruple screws driven by Parsons single-reduction-geared turbines: 72,000shp: $32\frac{1}{4}$ knots. Four Admiralty 3-drum boilers. There were five ships in the class of which four, LEANDER, ORION, NEPTUNE and ACHILLES formed the Second Cruiser Squadron, Home Fleet, and were the most modern ships present at the Review. (AJAX was still running trials). LEANDER went to the Royal New Zealand Navy in 1937. Her service during WWII was in the Pacific and the Far East and, for a time, she operated under the American Admiral Halsey. She was broken up in 1949.

25

26

25
NEPTUNE C. *Completed:* 1934 Details and description as for
LEANDER (Plate 24), but displacement was 7,030/9,740 tD. During WWII
she was first based at Freetown for convoy escort duties in the South Atlantic.
In May 1940 she went to reinforce Admiral Sir Andrew Cunningham's fleet at
Alexandria. Later she became the Flagship for Admiral John Cunningham for
the expedition to Duala to prevent the Vichy French from using the
Cameroons as a base. In early 1941 she went to Scapa to join the fleet there,
making sorties to try to intercept the German battleship BISMARCK. Later
that year she was sent to Malta and, with other ships, she escorted the fast
merchant ship MV *Breconshire*. While off Tripoli she struck two mines and
later, two more. These last two caused her suddenly to capsize and sink with
the loss of all but one of her ship's company.

26
ACHILLES C. *Completed:* 1932. Details and description as for
LEANDER (Plate 24) but displacement was 7,030/9,740 tD. She saw
extensive service during WWII but her main claim to fame was that she was
one of the three cruisers (EXETER, AJAX, ACHILLES) which defeated the
German 'Pocket Battleship' ADMIRAL GRAF SPEE (Plate 70) at the battle
of River Plate in December 1939. She was later lent to the Royal New Zealand
Navy and was at the battle of Guadalcanal (1942-3) and Okinawa (1945).
After the War she was refitted in Britain and then sold to the Royal Indian
Navy in 1948 being renamed DELHI. Here, ACHILLES is seen in a typical
Review setting with a large yacht passing through the lines.

27
STURDY D. *Completed:* 1919. (. ₁6×26¾×11) 1,075 tD. *Complement:*
98 officers and men. *Armament:* Three 4-inch and six smaller guns. Four
21-inch torpedo tubes in pairs amidships. This was one of the few remaining
S-Class destroyers of which 54 were built. They were very fast little ships and
had Brown-Curtis single-reduction-geared turbines driving twin screws. They
developed 27,000 shp for a speed of 36 knots. They each had three oil-fired
Yarrow boilers. At the Review, STURDY was acting as attendant destroyer to
the aircraft carrier COURAGEOUS and all her armament was removed.
During WWII she was re-armed and served as an inshore convoy escort but
was wrecked on Tiree Island off the west coast of Scotland, in October 1940
and became a total loss.

28
VALOROUS D (Built as F/L) Second Destroyer Flotilla, Home Fleet.
Completed: 1917. (312×29½×11) 1,325/1,480 tD. *Complement:* 134
officers and men. *Armament:* Four 4-inch and six smaller guns. Six 21-inch
torpedo tubes in two triple mountings. During and after WWI she was fitted as
a minelayer. *Propulsion:* Twin screws Brown Curtis single-reduction-geared
turbines, 27,000 shp: 32 knots. VALOROUS spent most of WWII as a
North Sea convoy escort. She was scrapped in 1948.

29

30

31

32

33

29
WINCHELSEA D Attached to Fifth Submarine Flotilla. *Completed:*
1918 (312×29½×11) 1,100/1,480 tD. *Armament:* Seen here as a
submarine tender, she had no armament. Later she was re-armed with four
4-inch and eight smaller guns including some AA. Six 21-inch torpedo tubes.
Propulsion: Brown-Curtis single-reduction-geared turbines: 27,000 shp twin
screws, 31 knots at full load. She was one of the famous 'W' Class destroyers
which, although more than 20 years old at the outbreak of WWII, gave an
excellent account of themselves. WINCHELSEA acquitted herself with
distinction at the Dunkirk evacuation and later was employed on North Sea
convoys. She survived the war in Europe and was broken up in 1945.

30
BEAGLE D. Fourth Destroyer Flotilla, Mediterranean Fleet. *Completed:*
1931 (323×32¼×8½) 1,360 tD. *Complement:* 138 officers and men.
Armament: Four 4.7-inch and seven smaller guns including two pompom AA.
Eight 21-inch torpedo tubes in quadruple mountings (The 'B's were the first
destroyers to have this feature). *Propulsion:* Twin screws powered by Parsons
single-reduction-geared turbines 34,000 shp: 35 knots. Three Admiralty
3-drum WT boilers working at 300 psi and with 600°F of superheat. These
were among the earliest RN ships to use high temperature superheated steam
but it was not then universally adopted. During WWII BEAGLE served with
the Home Fleet until 1941 when she became a Western Approaches escort
ship. In 1943 she came south and the next year took part in the Normandy
landings. She was broken up in 1946.

31
CRUSADER D. *Completed:* 1932 (326×33×8½ (mean)) 1,375 tD.
Complement: 145 officers and men. *Main armament:* four 4.7-inch guns.
Seven smaller guns. Eight 21-inch torpedo tubes. *Propulsion:* Twin screws
driven by Parsons single-reduction-geared turbines developing 36,000shp.
Maximum speed 35½ knots. Three oil-fired Admiralty 3-drum boilers. Soon
after the Review, CRUSADER was sold to Canada and became RCN
OTTAWA. During WWII she was on North Atlantic convoy escort duties. In
September 1940 while escorting outward bound convoy ON 127, she was
torpedoed and sunk in mid-Atlantic together with seven merchant ships of the
convoy.

32/33
FIREDRAKE (top) and FEARLESS (lower) were destroyers of the 'E' and
'F' classes with details and dimensions as for ECHO (Plate 34). They were
examples of the nine classes of destroyer completed between 1930 and 1938,
each class carrying names which commenced with the letters A to I
respectively. Except that there were only four 'C's each class was composed of
eight ships. They were fast, handsome and handy little ships which gave
wonderful service in WWII but with heavy losses. FIREDRAKE was
torpedoed and sunk by a U-boat in the North Atlantic in December 1942.
FEARLESS was bombed and sunk eighteen months earlier during convoy
duties in the Eastern Mediterranean in July 1941.

34

35

34
ECHO D. Fifth Destroyer Flotilla, Home Fleet. *Completed:* 1934
(329×33¼×8½) 1,375 tD. *Complement:* 145 Officers and men. *Armament:*
Four 4.7-inch and seven smaller guns. Two depth charge throwers aft. Eight
21-inch torpedo tubes in quadruple mounts. *Propulsion:* Twin screws:
Parsons single-reduction-geared turbines: 36,000 shp: 35½ knots. Three
Admiralty 3-drum boilers providing superheated steam at 300 psi. This was
one of the earlier examples of the use of superheated steam in the Royal Navy.
In ECHO and her sister ships the superheat temperature was moderate, a mere
200°F. This is interesting in view of the high superheats used in some earlier
ships (600°F in the 'A' and 'B' Classes of 1931.) It was not until 1939 that
higher pressures and superheats were generally adopted. ECHO saw service
during WWII in the Atlantic and was present at the hunting of the
BISMARCK. In the Mediterranean she took part in Malta convoys and then
was at the invasion of Sicily and Salerno. In the Aegean in November 1943,
she assisted in the landings and consequent evacuation of Leros. She was
transferred to the Greek Navy in 1944 and was renamed NAVARINON. She
was scrapped in 1956.

35
KEMPENFELT F/L Second Destroyer Flotilla, Home Fleet. *Completed:*
1932 (323×32¼×8½) 1,390 tD. *Armament:* Four 4.7-inch, one 3-inch HA
and eight smaller guns. Eight 21-inch torpedo tubes in quadruple mounts.
Propulsion: Twin screws driven by Parsons single-reduction-geared turbines:
36,000shp: 35½ knots. Three Admiralty 3-drum boilers with a working
pressure of 300 psi. In 1939 she was sold to Canada and became RCN
ASSINIBOINE. In the early months of the war she patrolled in the West
Indies area but spent most of WWII as an A/S destroyer on convoy protection
duties in the North Atlantic. In 1942 while on such duty she rammed and sank
a German U-boat. She was broken up in 1947.

36

37

36
HALCYON   Minesweeper (used for Fishery Protection in peace time)
Reserve Fleet. *Completed:* 1933   (230×33½×6½)   815 tD.   *Complement: 80*
Officers and men.   *Armament:* Two 4-inch, ten smaller guns.   *Propulsion:*
Twin screws driven by two 3-cylinder totally enclosed compound engines with
rotary cam poppet valves. 1,770 ihp: 16½ knots. There were thirteen ships in
the class, most with two sets of inward turning triple expansion engines
developing 2,000 hp for 17 knots. HALCYON survived the war and was
broken up in 1950.

37
GUARDIAN   Net-layer and Fleet Photographic Ship.   *Completed:* 1933
(310×53×11⅛)   2,860 tD.   *Complement:* 150 officers and men.   *Armament:*
Two 4-inch AA guns.   *Propulsion:* Parsons single-reduction-geared turbines
driving two screws: 6,500 shp: 18 knots.   Anti-submarine and anti-torpedo
nets are laid across the entrances to harbours and anchorages to protect the
ships within and the net-layer not only lays the nets but retrieves them for
relaying as required. There were two modern net layers, the sister ship to
GUARDIAN being PROTECTOR. The former worked mainly with the
Home Fleet during WWII while PROTECTOR spent much time at
Alexandria. Apart from her designed duties she also acted as a 'funeral ship'
carrying the bodies of dead men from damaged ships out into the
Mediterranean for burial at sea. GUARDIAN was scrapped in 1962.

38

39

38

KELLETT (ex UPPINGHAM) Surveying Vessel. (231×28½×7½) 800
tD. Built as an improved 'Hunt' Class minesweeper at Renfrew in 1919 but
was immediately converted (with three other similar ships) to a surveying
vessel. She had twin screws driven by two triple expansion engines giving her a
speed of 16 knots. She was a coal burner and had two Yarrow boilers. She was
armed with a 3-pounder gun. KELLETT was scrapped in 1945.

39

TITANIA Depot Ship, Submarines. *Completed:* 1915 as a merchant ship
(name unknown) and purchased by Admiralty the same year
(341×46½×18½) 5,250 tD. *Complement:* 249 officers and men. *Armament:*
Two torpedo tubes. *Armour:* None. *Propulsion:* Single screw : reciprocating
engine, coal burning, 14½ knots. Could be distinguished by her very tall
foremast. She served throughout WWII as a depot ship to various flotillas in
home waters, starting the war at Blyth and finishing at the Holy Loch. She was
broken up at Faslane in 1949.

40

H-32 Submarine. *Completed:* 1918 ($170 \times 15\frac{3}{4} \times 12\frac{1}{2}$) 410 tD.
Complement: 22 officers and men. *Armament:* One machine gun. Four
21-inch torpedo tubes. *Propulsion:* Twin screw: two 8-cylinder 4-cycle diesel
engines/electric motors when submerged: $13/10\frac{1}{2}$ knots. The three 'H' Class
were the smallest boats at the Review and, with five 'L' Class the oldest. H-32
was used for training but on the outbreak of WWII she became operational
and was attached to the Sixth Submarine Flotilla at Blyth. She was broken up
in 1944.

41

42

43

44

41
OXLEY S/M. *Completed:* 1927 (275×27¾×13½) 1,354/1,872 tD.
Complement: 54 officers and men. *Armament:* One 4-inch and two machine
guns. Six 21-inch bow and two 21-inch stern torpedo tubes. *Propulsion:* Twin
screw, diesels, 3,000 bhp for a surface speed of 15¼ knots. Electric motors,
1,350 bhp for submerged speed of 9 knots. OXLEY and OTWAY were built
for the Australian Navy but were given to the Royal Navy in 1931. They were
both equipped with net cutters over the bows. OXLEY was accidentally sunk
by the British S/M TRITON off Norway in September, 1939.

42
STURGEON S/M. *Completed:* 1932 (187×23½×10½) 640/927 tD.
Complement: 40 officers and men. *Armament:* One 3-inch and one machine
gun. Six 21-inch torpedo tubes. *Propulsion:* Twin screws: Diesel motors
1,550 ihp: 13¾ knots surface speed, electric motors 1,300 ihp: 10 knots
submerged. During WWII she served in the North Sea, the Arctic and the
North African campaign. In 1943 she was lent to the Royal Netherlands
Navy, being renamed ZEEHOND and returned to RN in 1945. She was
broken up in 1947.

43
PORPOISE S/M Minelayer. *Completed:* 1933 (267×29×13¾) 1,500/
2,060 tD. *Complement:* 55 officers and men. *Armament:* One 4-inch and
two machine guns. Six 21-inch torpedo tubes. *Propulsion:* She had twin
screws and was propelled on the surface by diesel motors of 3,300 bhp and by
electric motors of 1,630 bhp when submerged. Speeds were 15/8¾ knots. She
carried 50 mines. She and her five sisters were very successful boats and
during WWII PORPOISE saw service at Norway, in the Atlantic and in the
Mediterranean. Later she was attached to the Eastern Fleet and she was lost in
January 1945, probably by an aircraft attack.

44
At all naval reviews there are interesting merchant ships which provide for
their passengers grandstand views of events. Present among a number of
famous ships at the Review of 1935 was the Royal Mail Lines SS ATLANTIS
which, when completed in 1913, was named ANDES. She was a ship of
15,620 tons gross with triple screws, the wing shafts being driven by triple
expansion engines and the centre shaft by an exhaust steam turbine. Her speed
was 17 knots. She originally sailed on the Southampton-South American
service of the Company until 1915 when she became an armed merchant
cruiser (AMC) until the end of WWI. Working with the 10th Cruiser Squadron
with her sister ship ALCANTARA, in February 1916 she engaged the
German raider GREIF. ALCANTARA and GREIF were both sunk. In 1919,
ANDES returned to her prewar duties until 1930 when she was refitted as a
cruise liner, painted white and renamed ATLANTIS. She carried 450 first
class passengers and became a popular and well-loved ship. She was also
present at the 1937 Naval Review. During WWII she became a hospital ship
and, after the war, served as an emigrant ship to Australia and New Zealand.
She was broken up in 1952.

45

45
Among the smaller passenger ships at the Review of 1935 was the Yeoward
Line SS ALONDRA, a ship of 3,445 tons gross, built in 1922. She had a
single screw driven by a triple expansion engine and her speed was a
comfortable 12 knots. Her usual run was between Liverpool, Madeira and the
Canary Islands. In addition to her 120 passengers she carried general cargo
outward and bananas homeward. Many passengers made the round trip which
occupied about three weeks. This photograph shows her off Teneriffe when she
was homeward bound and a month before she was at the Review. She was sold
out of service in 1939.

Coronation Review 1937

King George V died on 20 January 1936 and was succeeded by his eldest son, Edward, Prince of Wales, who became King Edward VIII. For various reasons the reign of King Edward VIII was brief and he abdicated the throne on 12 December 1936 in favour of his brother Prince Albert who became King George VI. King Edward VIII was never crowned and so, the Coronation Review of the Fleet at Spithead on 20 May 1937 was carried out by King George VI accompanied by Queen Elizabeth (now the Queen Mother) with their two daughters.

Following in less than two years the Silver Jubilee Review of 1935, many ships of the Royal Navy were at both Reviews. In fact, out of 145 British and Empire warships assembled at Spithead in 1937, no fewer than 86 had been present at the 1935 Review. Of the capital ships, the most important change was the presence of the refitted Battle Cruiser REPULSE in place of RENOWN which, in 1937, was being refitted. The new cruisers SOUTHAMPTON and NEWCASTLE were also of great interest and their handsome appearance was the subject of much favourable comment. The presence of new submarines and of new destroyers of the 'G', 'H' and 'I' classes was very heartening to the many there who regarded war with Germany as inevitable.

At the Jubilee Review of 1935 there had been no foreign ships. In 1937, no fewer than 18 were present. They were of many types and classes ranging from the small Cruiser CUBA to the old American Battleship NEW YORK. Most impressive of all were the ships of Nazi Germany, France and Japan. From Germany came the 'pocket battleship' ADMIRAL GRAF SPEE a powerful and fast ship whose gunnery was known to be exceptionally accurate. She was one of the first warships to have diesel main engines. From France came the brand new Battleship DUNKERQUE, again an immensely powerful ship, in some ways resembling our NELSON and RODNEY. Japan sent one of her rebuilt cruisers, the ASIGARA, also a fast and heavily armed ship (but hardly a 'thing of beauty'). With hindsight it is of interest to recall that all of these great ships were destroyed by the British Navy during WW2.

Another feature of the 1937 Review was the fine array of great passenger liners. In 1935 there were 15 present; in 1937 there were 24! Most were 'floating grandstands' for their passengers, but five were earmarked for 'Government guests' and anchored off the head of the lines, after being in the 'procession' round the Fleet.

The King and Queen in the old Royal Yacht VICTORIA AND ALBERT were preceded through the lines by the Trinity House Yacht PATRICIA and followed by the Admiralty Yacht ENCHANTRESS. Every ship was 'manned' and 'three cheers' were called by each of the ships as the Royal Yacht passed by. After the Review, there was a fly-past of aircraft of the Fleet Air Arm and at night from 2200 to 2400 came the illuminations — 'the whole fleet was lit up!'

Next day, the King visited four of the major ships present and at 1400 hours the Royal Yacht returned to harbour at Portsmouth. The fleets dispersed and a very impressive and memorable occasion had ended.

Immediately preceding the Spithead Review in 1937, London had its own 'mini review' of the Fleet. From 7 to 13 May a representative selection of HM ships were at anchorages which stretched from the Upper Pool (HMS FLEETWOOD, EXMOUTH and RIN INDUS) to Southend (HMS COURAGEOUS, NELSON, RODNEY and the five 'Revenge' class battleships with attendant destroyers). The new cruisers SOUTHAMPTON and NEWCASTLE were, with HMS GUARDIAN and CRUSADER in Gravesend Reach and CAIRO was at Greenwich. The nine 'E' class destroyers of the Fifth Flotilla, Home Fleet, were at various anchorages and two were in Tilbury Dock as was HMS LUCIA (Depot ship — Submarines). Londoners, and many others, 'reviewed' the ships from private yachts and from the excellent and frequent excursions made by the Eagle and Queen Line Pleasure steamers. Happy days!

1937

HM Ship	Type	HM Ship	Type	HM Ship	Type	HM Ship	Type
ABERDEEN	E	FURIOUS	A/C	PROTECTOR	N.L.	STARFISH	S/M
ACHERON	D	GALATEA	C	PUFFIN	P	STRONGHOLD	D
ALRESFORD	M/S	GALLANT	D	QUEEN ELIZABETH	B/S	STURGEON	S/M
AMAZON	D	GARLAND	D	RAMILLIES	B/S	SWORDFISH	S/M
ANTELOPE	D	GIPSY	D	REPULSE	B/C	TEDWORTH	M/S
BARHAM	B/S	GLORIOUS	A/C	RESOLUTION	B/S	THAMES	S/M
BASILISK	D	GLOWWORM	D	REVENGE	B/S	TITANIA	S.M.D.S.
BEAGLE	D	GRAFTON	D	RODNEY	B/S	TYRANT	D
BLANCHE	D	GRAMPUS	S/M	RORQUAL	S/M	VANQUISHER	D
BOADICIA	D	GRENADA	D	ROYAL OAK	B/S	VERITY	D
BOREAS	D	GRENVILLE	F/L	ROYAL SOVEREIGN	B/S	VIDETTE	D
BRAMBLELEAF	O/T	GREYHOUND	D	SAGUENAY	D	VISCOUNT	D
BRAZEN	D	GRIFFIN	D	SALAMANDER	M/S	WALPOLE	D
BRILLIANT	D	GUARDIAN	N.L.	SALTBURN	M/S	WANDERER	D
BROKE	F/L	H34	S/M	SARDONYX	D	WHITSHED	D
BULLDOG	D	H43	S/M	SEAHORSE	S/M	WILD SWAN	D
CAIRO	C	H49	S/M	SEAWOLF	S/M	WINCHELSEA	D
CARDIFF	C	H50	S/M	SEVERN	S/M	WINCHESTER	D
CARLISLE	C	HALCYON	M/S	SHROPSHIRE	C	WISHART	D
CLYDE	S/M	HAREBELL	F.P.V.	SKATE	D	WOLFHOUND	D
CODRINGTON	F/L	HARRIER	M/S	SKEENA	D	WOOLSTON	D
COLOMBO	C	HEREWARD	D	SKIPJACK	M/S	WOOLWICH	R/S
COMET	D	HERMES	A/C	SOUTHAMPTON	C	WREN	D
COURAGEOUS	A/C	HOOD	B/C	SPEARFISH	S/M	WRESTLER	D
COVENTRY	C	HUSSAR	M/S	SPEEDWELL	M		
CRUSADER	D	ICARUS	D				
CURACOA	C	IMOGEN	D				
CURLEW	C	INDUS	E				
CYCLOPS	S.M.D.S	IRON DUKE	Tr.S				
DEVONSHIRE	C	KELLETT	S/S				
DUNEDIN	C	KEMPENFELT	F/L	**Foreign Warships**			
ECHO	D	KITTIWAKE	P	Ship		Type	Country
ECLIPSE	D	L26	S/M				
ELECTRA	D	L27	S/M	MORENO		B/S	Argentina
ENCOUNTER	D	L54	S/M	CUBA		C	Cuba
ESCAPADE	D	LEANDER	C	NIELS IUEL		ARM. SHIP	Denmark
ESCORT	D	LONDON	C	KALEV		S/M	Estonia
ESK	D	LUCIA	S.M.D.S.	VÄINÄMÖINEN		ARM. SHIP	Finland
EXMOUTH	F/L	LUPIN	E	DUNKERQUE		B/S	France
EXPRESS	D	MALLARD	P	ADMIRAL GRAF SPEE		B/S	Germany
FAME	D	NARWHAL	S/M	GIORGIOS AVEROFF		C	Greece
FAULKNOR	F/L	NELSON	B	ASIGARA		C	Japan
FEARLESS	E	NEWCASTLE	C	JAVA		C	Netherlands
FLEETWOOD	E	NIGER	M/S	BARTOLOMEU DIAS		S	Portugal
FLINDERS	S/S	OBERON	S/M	BURZA		D	Poland
FORESIGHT	D	OXLEY	S/M	REGINA MARIA		D	Romania
FOXHOUND	D	PEGASUS	A/C	CISCAR		D	Spain
FROBISHER	C	PORPOISE	S/M	DROTTNING VICTORIA		ARM. SHIP	Sweden
				KOCATEPE		D	Turkey
				NEW YORK		B/S	USA
				MARAT		B/S	USSR

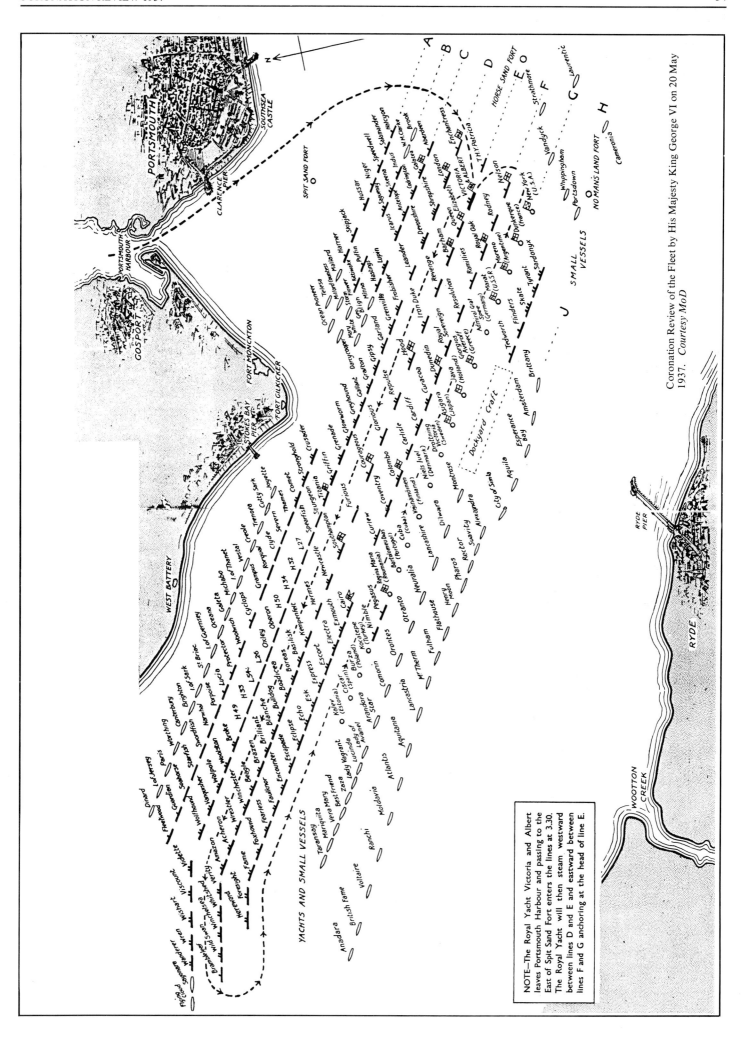

Coronation Review of the Fleet by His Majesty King George VI on 20 May 1937. *Courtesy MoD*

NOTE—The Royal Yacht Victoria and Albert leaves Portsmouth Harbour and passing to the East of Spit Sand Fort enters the lines at 3.30. The Royal Yacht will then steam westward between lines D and E and eastward between lines F and G anchoring at the head of line E.

46

47

46

HERMES A/C Reserve Fleet. *Completed:* 1924 (598×70) (90ft over flight deck) ×18¾) 10,850/13,000 tD. *Complement:* 748 officers and men including flying personnel. Could carry up to 21 aircraft. *Armament:* Six 5.5-inch, three 4-inch AA, 18 smaller guns. *Armour:* 3-inch main belts, 1-inch deck. *Propulsion:* Twin screws driven by Parsons single-reduction-geared turbines: 40,000 shp: 25 knots. HERMES was the first British aircraft carrier to be originally designed and built as such. During WWII her most important role was in the first attack on the French battleship RICHELIEU at Dakar in 1940 when her torpedo bombers caused severe damage. She later took part in the East African Campaign, her aircraft attacking the Italian base at Mogadishu. In 1942 she was sent to Trincomalee, Ceylon, with a small force of ships to discourage the Japanese from attacking Ceylon. However, in April of that year, while off Ceylon, she was attacked by Japanese aircraft and after receiving nearly 40 bomb hits, she sank.

47

GLORIOUS A/C Mediterranean Fleet. *Completed* as a cruiser 1917. Converted to A/C 1924-30. *Complement:* (Including flying personnel) 1,216 officers and men. Principal dimensions and details as for COURAGEOUS (Plate 16). Like COURAGEOUS, GLORIOUS was an early casualty of WWII. After a short period in the Indian Ocean, she joined the Home Fleet and took part in the Norwegian Campaign in 1940, ferrying fighter aircraft to Narvik. While taking part in these operations on 8 June, 1940, she was surprised by the German Battleship SCHARNHORST and was sunk by gunfire before it was possible to launch her torpedo-carrying aircraft. Her casualties were very severe, only three officers and thirty-five men being rescued nearly three days after the action.

48

BARHAM B/S Flagship, First Battle Squadron, Mediterranean Fleet.
Completed: 1915. Specification and details as for VALIANT (Plate 4). Soon
after commissioning, BARHAM and WARSPITE were in collision during
Fleet exercises but both ships were present at Jutland the next year. BARHAM
was damaged during the battle and had some men killed and wounded. With
the other four battleships of the 'Queen Elizabeth' Class she was extensively
refitted during the period 1925-1933 but, alone of the five ships, owing to the
outbreak of WWII she was never extensively modernised and reconstructed.
At the outbreak of WWII the ship was in the Mediterranean Fleet based at
Alexandria but in November 1939 she joined the Home Fleet and her first duty
was, with other ships, to screen the first Canadian troop convoy. While still in
the North Atlantic at the end of December she was torpedoed by a U-boat and
was under repair for three months. In November 1940 she went to the Eastern
Mediterranean and was at the Battle of Matapan and later at the battle for
Crete during which she was damaged by a bomb. However, the end came on
25 November 1941 when she was hit by several torpedoes from the German
submarine U331. The old ship blew up with the loss of 862 officers and men.

HOOD B/C Flagship, Battle Cruiser Squadron, Mediterranean Fleet. For
dimensions and details see Plate 13. When painted in the lighter grey of the
Mediterranean Fleet, the beautiful proportions of this great ship were greatly
enhanced. During the early part of WWII, however, HOOD was with the
Home Fleet and steamed many miles in Northern waters in an effort to
intercept any units of the German battle fleet endeavouring to break out into
the Atlantic. She also protected convoys to Narvik. In June 1940 with the
aircraft carrier ARK ROYAL she joined Force H at Gibraltar and became the
Flagship of Admiral Somerville. While based at Gibraltar she played a major
part in the destruction of the French fleet at Oran. However, in December
1940 she was again at Scapa hunting German capital ships, protecting
convoys and patrolling northern waters, often in the foulest weather. In May
1941 the German Battleship BISMARCK with the heavy cruiser PRINZ
EUGEN were spotted by the cruiser SUFFOLK steaming into the Atlantic
through the Denmark Strait. HOOD and the new battleship PRINCE OF
WALES joined the 8-inch cruisers NORFOLK and SUFFOLK and gave
chase. The German ships were engaged and in the ensuing battle HOOD was
hit by a salvo from BISMARCK and blew up with the loss of all but three of
her ship's company — 1,419 officers and men.

50

51

50

REPULSE B/C. *Completed:* 1916. See also RENOWN (Plate 14)
($794\frac{1}{4} \times 102\frac{3}{4} \times 26\frac{3}{4}$) 32,000/37,400 tD. *Complement:* About 1,200 officers
and men. *Armament:* Six 15-inch, twelve 4-inch, eight 4-inch AA and other
smaller guns. Two torpedo tubes. *Armour:* As for RENOWN. Anti-torpedo
bulges. *Propulsion:* She had quadruple screws driven by Brown-Curtis direct
drive turbines developing 112,000 shp: $31\frac{1}{2}$ knots. REPULSE received her
major refit during 1932-36 but this was not so extensive as that provided for
RENOWN (1936-39) and she was not re-engined. She also had less anti-
aircraft armament. During WWII she served with the Home Fleet until 1941
when, with PRINCE OF WALES, she was transferred to the Eastern Fleet.
On 10 December 1941, both ships were attacked by Japanese torpedo
bombers and first REPULSE and then PRINCE OF WALES were sunk.

51

REPULSE. Midships view showing 4-inch guns in triple mountings. This
arrangement of a group of three guns was awkward and the gun crew of 23
men got in each other's way. Surprisingly, these guns were not removed during
her 1936-39 refit. Had she been provided with more anti-aircraft armament the
result of her battle with Japanese torpedo bombers might have been different.

52
CURLEW   Anti-aircraft Cruiser   10th Cruiser Squadron, Reserve Fleet.
Soon after her appearance at the Jubilee Review of 1935 CURLEW (with her
sister ship COVENTRY) was completely re-armed as an anti-aircraft ship
being given 10 4-inch AA guns in single mountings and 12 smaller guns. Her
torpedo tubes were removed. During WWII she was in action during the
Norwegian campaign but she was bombed and sunk by German aircraft off
Narvik on 26 May 1940.

53
SOUTHAMPTON   C   Flagship   Second Cruiser Squadron, Home Fleet.
Completed: 1937 (Three months before appearing at the Review).
$(591\frac{1}{2} \times 61\frac{3}{4} \times 17)$ 9,100 tD.   *Complement:* 700 officers and men.   *Armament:*
12 6-inch guns in triple turrets, the centre gun in each turret was mounted
further back than the two outer guns. It was found that with all guns in line the
blast of the three guns firing together could deflect the accuracy of the
projectile. Secondary armament consisted of eight 4-inch AA and 18 smaller
guns. She had six 21-inch torpedo tubes in triple mounts and carried three
aircraft in a hangar abaft the bridge with a catapult between the funnels.
Armour: 4-inch side armour and 2-inch on turrets.   *Propulsion:* Quadruple
screws were powered by Parsons single-reduction-geared turbines developing
75,000 shp for 32 knots.   SOUTHAMPTON and her sisters were probably
the best looking ships in the Navy, their raking funnels and masts giving them
a particularly 'dashing' appearance when travelling fast at sea. The service of
SOUTHAMPTON during WWII was tragically brief. Working in Northern
waters with the Home Fleet during the early part of the war she then went to
the Mediterranean in 1940 and took part in the protection of troop convoys
from Gibraltar to Alexandria and to Malta. It was while on these duties in
January 1941 that SOUTHAMPTON received a direct hit with a 1,000 lb
bomb from a Stuka. This set the ship on fire and she had to be sunk by our
own forces.

54
SOUTHAMPTON   C   Midship view showing aircraft cranes, hangar,
conning tower and bridge and 'B' turret.

55

56

55
NEWCASTLE C Second Cruiser Squadron, Home Fleet. *Completed:*
1937. Dimensions and details as for SOUTHAMPTON (Plate 54).
NEWCASTLE had a very busy time during WWII. She was first with the
Home Fleet and took part in the many convoys, patrols, and interceptions
during the first years of the war. June 1942 saw her in the Eastern
Mediterranean and soon after she was damaged by a torpedo from an E-boat
while on convoy escort duty. She was later to serve with the Eastern Fleet and
in the East Indies. Her final war duty was during the Korean war of 1952-53.
She was broken up in 1959.

56
LONDON C Flagship First Cruiser Squadron, Mediterranean Fleet. Her
description is identical in all main details with those of the other two ships in
the Squadron, SHROPSHIRE and DEVONSHIRE (Plates 17 and 18). At
the outbreak of WWII, LONDON was in Chatham Dockyard undergoing a
major reconstruction. She emerged in 1941 as a two-funnelled cruiser with an
aircraft hangar abaft the bridge and in appearance not unlike a 'Colony' Class
cruiser. After a working-up period during which she intercepted three German
supply ships in the South Atlantic, she worked in Northern waters providing
cover for several convoys to Russia. In 1944 she went to the Eastern Fleet and
played a major part in the rehabilitation by the Allies of the territories
conquered by the Japanese. Still in the Far East in 1949 she tried to assist
AMETHYST in taking supplies up the Yangtze to a British colony.
AMETHYST succeeded but LONDON was driven back by shore-based guns
and was badly damaged. She limped home to Chatham where she de-
commissioned before being broken up at Barrow in 1950.

57

58

57
GALATEA C Flagship of Rear Admiral Commanding Destroyers.
Completed: 1935 (480×51×13¾) 5,220 tD. *Complement:* 450 officers and men. *Armament:* Six 6-inch, eight 4-inch AA and nine smaller guns. Six 21-inch torpedo tubes. One aircraft on catapult between the funnels. *Armour:* 2-inch side armour with 1-inch on turrets. *Propulsion:* Quadruple screws, single-reduction-geared turbines with cruising turbines. 64,000 shp: 32½ knots. The second of four light cruisers of the 'Arethusa' class. During WWII she worked, first, with the Home Fleet and then, in 1941, in the Eastern Mediterranean. She was torpedoed and sunk by a U-boat off Alexandria in December 1941.

58
AMAZON D Tenth Destroyer Flotilla, Reserve Fleet. *Completed:* 1926 (322×31×8½) 1,352 tD. *Complement:* 138 officers and men. *Armament:* Four 4.7-inch and six smaller guns. Six 21-inch torpedo tubes in triple mounts. *Propulsion:* Twin screws driven by Brown-Curtis single-reduction-geared turbines each consisting of a high-pressure and a low-pressure cruising stage. Three Admiralty 3-drum boilers with superheaters. 39,500 shp: 37 knots. This ship was largely designed by the builders — Sir John Thornycroft and Co. During WWII she spent most of her time with the Home Fleet and in the Western Approaches but she was damaged when acting as escort to a Russian convoy in March 1942. Thereafter she became a training ship until being broken up in 1948.

59

60

61

59

WHITSHED D 10th Destroyer Flotilla, Reserve Fleet. *Completed:* 1919 (312×29½×10¾) 1,120 tD. *Complement:* 134 officers and men. *Armament:* Four 4.7-inch, two 2-pdr pompom and five smaller guns. Six 21-inch torpedo tubes. This was one of the modified 'W' Class destroyers built after WWI. *Propulsion:* They had two screws driven by single-reduction-geared turbines developing 27,000 shp for 34 knots. WHITSHED gave splendid service during the evacuation of Dunkirk but for most of WWII she was engaged in convoy protection duties off the East coast of Britain. She was broken up in 1948.

60

VISCOUNT D Ninth Destroyer Flotilla, Reserve Fleet. *Completed:* 1917 (312×30½×10¾) 1,120 tD. *Complement:* 134 officers and men. *Armament:* Four 4-inch, one 2-pdr pompom and five smaller guns. Six 21-inch torpedo tubes. She was one of two Thornycroft 'V' Class destroyers, the other being VICEROY. *Propulsion:* Twin screws were powered by Brown-Curtis single-reduction-geared turbines developing 30,000 shp for 35 knots. During WWII her duties were as a convoy escort but in 1943 she was reconstructed as a long

range destroyer escort. One boiler and her forward funnel were removed to provide extra bunker space and her forecastle gun was replaced by a Hedgehog ahead-throwing A/S weapon. She retained two 4-inch guns but her anti-aircraft armament was increased. Her speed was reduced to 24 knots. She was broken up in 1947.

61

ACHERON D Tenth Destroyer Flotilla, Reserve Fleet. *Completed:* 1931 (323×32¼×8½) 1,350 tD. *Complement:* 138 officers and men. *Armament:* Four 4.7-inch and six smaller guns. Eight 21-inch torpedo tubes in quadruple mounts. She was equipped with high speed minesweeping gear aft. *Propulsion:* Twin screws driven by Parsons single-reduction-geared turbines: 34,000 shp: 35 knots. ACHERON had three Admiralty 3-drum WT boilers working at 500 psi and supplying superheated steam at 750°F. This was the first ship in the Royal Navy to operate with steam at such high pressure and temperature, neither of which was exceeded or even equalled for many years. She was a successful, fast and economical ship. Her record during WWII was brief as she was sunk by a mine off the Isle of Wight in December 1940.

62

63

62
LUCIA Depot ship for the Second Submarine Flotilla, Home Fleet.
$(367\frac{1}{2} \times 45\frac{1}{4} \times 18\frac{3}{4})$ 5,800 tD. *Complement:* 262 officers and men.
Armament: Two 3-pdr AA. No armour. This ship was originally the
Hamburg-Amerika SPREEWALD and was captured during WW1
(September 1914) by HMS BERWICK. She had been built in Hamburg in
1907 and was converted to a depot ship in 1916. *Propulsion:* Single screw
driven by a triple expansion engine. Speed was $12\frac{1}{2}$ knots. She burned coal.
She is shown here alongside the coaling dock at Tilbury. She was taking part in
the 'mini review' on the Thames a week before proceeding to Spithead (see
page 35). She was sold in 1948 and became the Merchant ship SINAI but was
scrapped three years later.

63
INDUS Escort Sloop ('Grimsby' Class) Royal Indian Navy. *Completed:*
1930 $(296\frac{1}{2} \times 35\frac{1}{2} \times 8\frac{1}{4})$ 1,190 tD. *Complement:* 119 officers and men.
Armament: Two 4.7-inch and fifteen smaller guns. *Propulsion:* Twin screws:
Parsons impulse/reaction single-reduction-geared turbines: 2,000 shp:
$16\frac{1}{2}$ knots. This was one of a very useful group of small ships which could be
used as convoy escorts or for fishery protection duties. During WWII some of
them were used as mine sweepers. INDUS was sunk off the coast of Burma by
Japanese dive bombers in April 1942.

64

65

64
MORENO Argentine B/S. *Completed:* 1915 (585×95×28 max))
27,720/31,500 tD. *Complement:* 1,215 officers and men. *Armament:*
Twelve 12-inch guns in twin turrets, the two forward turrets and the two after
turrets conventionally disposed, the midships turrets situated *en echelon* abaft
the forward funnel on the starboard side and one forward of the after funnel on
the port side. Her secondary armament was composed of twelve 6-inch guns in
barbettes and there were 18 smaller guns. Two submerged torpedo tubes.
Armour: 11-inch belt; 12-inch on turrets and conning tower. Lighter armour
elsewhere. *Propulsion:* Triple screws powered by Curtis single-reduction-
geared turbines: 45,000 shp: 23 knots.   Originally a coal burner; converted to
oil fuel during 1924-25 refit. The heavy lattice foremast proclaimed her United
States parentage! MORENO was broken up in 1957.

65
NEW YORK USA B/S. *Completed:* 1914 (573×106×26) 27,000/
30,000 tD. *Complement:* 1,314 officers and men. *Armament:* Ten 14-inch
guns in twin turrets, four turrets in the A, B, X, Y positions and one abaft the
funnel. Sixteen 5-inch and 24 smaller guns. She carried three aircraft and had a
catapult launcher atop the midships turret. *Armour:* 12-inch belt and conning
tower; 14-inch turrets; 12-inch barbettes. Lighter armour elsewhere. Anti-
torpedo bulges. *Propulsion:* Twin screws driven by two 4-cylinder triple
expansion engines: 28,100 shp: 19 knots.   She had an extensive refit in
1926-27 during which she was converted from coal to oil burning. During
WWI she was attached to the Grand Fleet 1917–18. She was broken up in
1947.

66

67

66
MARAT Russia Battleship. *Completed:* 1914 (619×87×27½) 23,206/26,400 tD. *Complement:* 1,125. *Armament:* 12 12-inch guns in four triple turrets. 16 4.7-inch and 15 smaller guns. Four 18-inch submerged torpedo tubes. One seaplane. No catapult. *Armour:* 8¾-inch belts; 12-inch turrets. Lighter armour in other areas. *Propulsion:* Quadruple screws driven by direct drive Parsons turbines: 42,000shp: 23 knots. Her boilers had dual firing — coal and oil on the German system. The forward funnel was bent backwards to prevent funnel gases invading the bridge and conning tower. MARAT was heavily damaged in 1941 by bombing at Kronstadt during WWII and she became a constructive total loss.

67
MARAT. Showing her bridge, 'bent' fore funnel, five of her 4.7-inch guns and three of her four 12-inch turrets.

68

DUNKERQUE France Battleship. *Completed*: 1937 (only five weeks
before the Review). (702×101¾×28) 26,500/33,000 tD. *Complement*: 1,381
officers and men. *Armament*: Eight 13-inch guns in quadruple turrets, 16
5.1-inch HA/LA and 44 smaller AA guns. Four aircraft or two flying boats
with catapult on the quarterdeck. *Armour*: 11-inch belt; 14-inch turrets and
conning tower; 7-inch deck. Lighter armour elsewhere. *Propulsion*:
Quadruple screws driven by Parsons single-reduction-geared turbines:
100,000 shp: 29½ knots. (On trials she developed 139,000 shp for 31½ knots).
Six Indret WT boilers. DUNKERQUE and her sister ship STRASBOURG
followed in some respects the design of NELSON and RODNEY but her two
main turrets each with four guns, replaced the three triple turrets in the British
ships. During WWII before the fall of France, DUNKERQUE formed part of
the hunting force looking for German raiders (eg ADMIRAL SCHEER) in the
South Atlantic. After the fall of France it was essential to the British that
French battleships did not fall into the hands of the Germans. Orders were
therefore given that if the ships would not join Britain or be demilitarised, they
were to be destroyed. With the refusal of the French to accept British terms,
the great ships were destroyed as they lay in harbour at Mers-el-Kebir.
DUNKERQUE was repaired sufficiently to sail, later to Toulon, where she
was scuttled and dismantled.

69

DUNKERQUE View showing two quadruple 5.1-inch gun turrets, aircraft
crane, hangar and catapult on the quarter-deck.

69

70

71

70
ADMIRAL GRAF SPEE Germany Armoured Ship ('Pocket Battleship').
Completed: 1936 ($609\frac{1}{4} \times 70\frac{3}{4} \times 21\frac{3}{4}$) 10,000 tD. *Complement:* 926 officers
and men. *Armament:* Six 11-inch guns in triple turrets; eight 5.9-inch; six
4.1-inch AA and 18 smaller guns. Eight 21-inch torpedo tubes. Two aircraft
with catapult abaft the bridge. *Armour:* 4-inch belt and turrets; $1\frac{1}{2}$-$2\frac{1}{4}$-inch
deck armour with 5-inch armour on conning tower and lighter armour
elsewhere. Anti-torpedo bulges. There were three ships in the class,
DEUTSCHLAND and ADMIRAL SCHEER being the other two.
Propulsion: They were the largest warships in the world to be propelled by
diesel engines. In ADMIRAL GRAF SPEE, the twin screws were driven by
eight MAN 8-cylinder 2-cycle double-acting engines, four geared to each shaft
through Vulkan clutches. 54,000 shp: 26 knots. It is reported that her engines
were not always reliable.

Some days before the outbreak of WWII, ADMIRAL GRAF SPEE, with
her supply ship, had already taken up station in the South Atlantic and she was
therefore immediately available to capture or sink Allied shipping on the trade
routes. She had considerable success. Eight groups of British and French
warships were organised to hunt down this raider and others known to be at
work. Finally, the 6-inch cruisers AJAX and ACHILLES accompanied by the
8-inch cruiser EXETER sighted the German ship off the River Plate on
13 December 1939 and a battle ensued. After damage had been sustained by
all the ships, ADMIRAL GRAF SPEE sought refuge in neutral waters and
entered the harbour of Montevideo. Four days later she left harbour and when
clear, blew herself up and sank.

71
ADMIRAL GRAF SPEE Midship view showing secondary armament,
control tower, searchlight platform on funnel and seaplane on catapult.

72

73

72
DROTTNING VICTORIA Sweden Battleship. *Completed:* 1918
(396¾×61×22 (max)) 7,120 tD. *Complement:* 450 officers and men.
Armament: Four 11-inch, eight 6-inch, four 3-inch AA and 11 smaller guns.
Armour: 8-inch belt and 11-inch turrets. Lighter armour elsewhere.
Propulsion: Twin screws driven by Westinghouse single-reduction-geared
turbines: 22,000 shp: 22½ knots. She had six boilers which were fired with oil
and coal and two oil-fired boilers. She had major refits in 1927 and in 1934-35.
She had an ice-breaking bow. DROTTNING VICTORIA was broken up in
1958.

73
VÄINÄMÖINEN Finland Coast Defence Ship. *Completed:* 1930
(305×55½×14¼) 3,900 tD. *Complement:* 330 officers and men. *Armament:*
Four 10-inch guns in twin turrets, eight 4.1-inch AA in twin turrets and four
2-pdr AA guns. *Armour:* 4-inch belt and turrets *Propulsion:* Twin screws:
diesel/electric drive: 5,000 bhp: 15½ knots. VÄINÄMÖINEN and her sister
ship ILMARINEN were strengthened for ice and had ice-breaking bows.

74

75

74
AVEROFF (ex GEORGIOS AVEROFF '35) Greece Armoured Cruiser.
Completed: 1910 (462×69×24¾ (max)) 9,450 tD. *Complement:* 550
officers and men. *Armament:* Four 9.2-inch, eight 7.5-inch and 18 smaller
guns. *Armour:* Very heavily armoured with 8-inch belt and 6½-7-inch on
turrets, barbettes and conning tower. *Propulsion:* She is a coal-burning ship
with twin screws driven by two 4-cylinder triple expansion engines,
19,000 shp: 22½ knots. AVEROFF was built in Italy but, when new, was sold
to Greece as a result of £300,000 being left to the Greek Navy by Georgios
Averoff, a millionaire. She had a very complete refit in France in 1925-27 and
her three torpedo tubes were removed. She was present at the Spithead Naval
Review of 1911 and again at that of 1937. She escaped with other units of the
RHN to Alexandria when the Germans occupied Greece during WWII and
became an accommodation and training ship there for most of the war. As a
result of Communist influence in Greece towards the end of the war, in April
1944, the crew of the AVEROFF mutinied and had to be subdued by loyal
Greek sailors from Alexandria. After the war in 1951 the old cruiser was
disposed of by RHN but was preserved and is now moored beside the Naval
School on the Island of Poros.

75
NIELS IUEL Denmark Coastal Defence Ship. *Completed:* 1918
(295¼×55½×15¾) 3,800 tD. *Complement:* 365 officers and men.
Armament: 10 5.9-inch in single mountings and 26 smaller guns. Two
17¾-inch torpedo tubes. *Armour:* 7¾-inch belts; 6¼-inch to conning tower.
Lighter armour elsewhere including 2½-inch deck armour. *Propulsion:* Twin
screws driven by triple expansion engines. 6,000 ihp: 16 knots. Four boilers,
two of which were coal fired. This ship was laid down in 1914, completed
1918 and first commissioned in 1923, the delays, presumably, being due to
WWI. She was modernised and refitted in 1935-36 and was then used as a
training ship. She was again militarised in 1940 but was captured by the
Germans. She was ultimately bombed and sunk by Russian aircraft at Kotka
in 1944.

76

77

78

79

80

76

JAVA Netherlands Cruiser. *Completed:* 1925 $(509\frac{1}{2} \times 52\frac{1}{2} \times 18 \text{ (max)})$
6,670 tD. *Complement:* 525 (including 240 Javanese). *Armament:* 10
5.9-inch, eight 40mm AA and 10 smaller guns. Two aircraft. She could carry
12 mines. *Armour:* 3-inch belt, 5-inch conning tower. Lighter armour
elsewhere. *Propulsion:* Triple screws driven by Krupp-Germania single-
reduction-geared turbines: 72,000 shp: 31 knots. Eight boilers. In WWII
JAVA formed part of a combined striking force with American and British
ships. In the Battle of the Java Sea, in February 1942, the British cruiser
EXETER and the destroyer ENCOUNTER were sunk and JAVA blew up
after being hit by torpedoes from the Japanese cruisers NATI and HAGURO
(Plate 77).

77

ASIGARA (ASHIGARA) Japan First Class Cruiser Flagship.
Completed: 1929, extensively rebuilt and re-armed 1934 $(640 \times 62\frac{1}{4} \times 16\frac{1}{2})$
10,000/12,700 tD. *Complement:* 692 officers and men. *Armament:* 10
8-inch eight 4.7-inch AA and ten smaller guns. Eight 21-inch torpedo tubes.
Four aircraft with two catapults. *Armour:* 3-inch belt, also deck and turrets.
Propulsion: Quadruple screws powered by single-reduction-geared turbines:
100,000 shp for 33 knots. There were four ships in the class, the others being
NATI, MYOKO and HAGURO. Only one, the MYOKO survived WWII;
ASIGARA was torpedoed and sunk by HM Submarine TRENCHANT off
Sumatra in June 1945.

78

ASIGARA Showing conning tower, funnels and AA guns.

79

KOCATEPE Turkey Destroyer. *Completed:* 1931 $(328\frac{1}{4} \times 30\frac{1}{4} \times 9\frac{1}{2})$
1,250/1,650 tD. *Complement:* 150 officers and men. *Armament:* Four
4.7-inch and four smaller guns. Six torpedo tubes in triple mounts.
Propulsion: Twin sc, Parsons single-reduction-geared turbines: 40,000 shp: 38
knots. Three WT boilers with superheaters. KOCATEPE and her sister ship
ADATEPE were named after the mountains above Izmir in which Kemal
Ataturk won a famous victory. The P&O ship seen behind KOCATEPE is the
SS COMORIN. KOCATEPE was sunk off Cyprus in 1974 by bombing from
Turkish aircraft!

80

BURZA Poland Destroyer. *Completed:* 1930 $(351 \times 29 \times 9\frac{3}{4})$
1,540 tD. *Complement:* 138 officers and men. *Armament:* Four 5.1-inch and
six smaller guns. Six 21-inch torpedo tubes. *Propulsion:* Twin screws driven
by single-reduction-geared Parsons turbines developing 35,000 shp: 33 knots.
BURZA escaped from Poland before the Nazi occupation and served with the
Royal Navy during WWII. It is now reported that the old ship has been
converted into a museum and moored in the harbour of Gdynia.

81

82

81

CUBA Cuba Cruiser. *Completed:* 1911 (260×39×14) 2,055 tD.
Armament: Two 4-inch, six 3-inch and 10 smaller guns. *Propulsion:* Single
screw driven by a triple expansion engine of 6,000 ihp for 18 knots. Two
oil-fired Foster-Wheeler boilers. A most interesting ship which had been
reconstructed during 1936-37 and completed just before the Review. Before
reconstruction she had a ram, two funnels, two tall pole masts and burned
coal. In 1956 she was again reconstructed and modernised, her tripod mast
being replaced by a shorter pole mast and being given more anti-aircraft guns
and two depth charge throwers. She was discarded in 1971.

82

BARTOLOMEU DIAS Portugal Sloop. *Completed:* 1935
($326\frac{3}{4}$×$44\frac{1}{4}$×$12\frac{1}{2}$) 1,816/2,478 tD. *Complement:* 189. *Armament:* Four
4.7-inch, two 3-inch AA and four smaller guns. Two depth charge throwers.
Can be used as a minelayer. One aircraft. *Propulsion:* Twin sc, Parsons
single-reduction-geared turbines, 8,000 shp: 21 knots. She was the largest
ship in the Portuguese Navy and was present again at the Naval Review at
Spithead in 1953.

83

84

83
REGINA MARIA Romania D. *Completed:* 1930 (334½×31½×11½)
1,900 tD. *Complement:* 212. *Armament:* Five 4.7-inch, one 3-inch AA, two
2-pdr pompom guns. Six 21-inch torpedo tubes. She also carried 50 mines.
Propulsion: Parsons single-reduction-geared turbines: 48,000 shp: 35 knots.
She was one of two destroyers built in Italy to a Thornycroft design which
accounts for her very British appearance.

84
The Orient Lines SS OTRANTO was photographed passing the destroyer
HMS ENCOUNTER as she steamed slowly towards her 'grandstand
anchorage' which was next to her sister ship ORONTES. OTRANTO was a
passenger liner of 19,970 tG. Completed in 1929 for the UK-Australia service.
She had single-reduction-geared turbines of 20,000 shp driving twin screws
and giving her a speed of 20 knots. She was a troopship during WWII and was
not broken up until 1962. ENCOUNTER was serving with the Fifth
Destroyer Flotilla Home Fleet. She was of 1,250 tD. Completed in 1934. She
had twin screws driven by Parsons single-reduction-geared turbines of
36,000 shp for 36 knots. She had four 4.7-inch guns and six smaller. Eight
21-inch torpedo tubes and two depth charge throwers. She was sunk by gunfire
in the Java Sea on 1 March, 1942.

85

86

85

AQUITANIA. *Completed:* 1914   901ft long ×97¼ft beam   45,647 tG.
Quadruple screws driven by Parsons direct drive turbines: 162,000 shp:
23 knots. Passengers: 3,230 in three classes.   Prominent among the 23 large
passenger liners present at the Review was the Cunard SS AQUITANIA —
the last of the great four-funnelled transatlantic liners. She was the grandstand
for over 1,500 passengers, many of them Americans. AQUITANIA had a
distinguished career during WWI as Armed Merchant Cruiser, Troop
Transport and, finally, Hospital Ship. During WWII she was one of the most
successful 'troopers' and carried many thousands of American soldiers and
airmen eastwards, returning many of them to the USA immediately after the
war. On the North Atlantic, in peacetime, she was a comfortable and much
loved ship, which, though fast, was never a Blue Riband contender. She was
broken up in 1950.

86

SS VANDYCK was a cruise liner owned by Lamport & Holt of Liverpool.
She was 559ft long with a beam of 64¼ft. Her gross tonnage was 13,233. She
had twin screws driven by single-reduction-geared turbines developing 7,000
shp for 14½ knots.   She was built for the New York-River Plate service of the
company, but after the loss of the Company's ship VECTRIS the trade fell off
and VANDYCK and her sister VOLTAIRE were laid up. In 1932 the two
ships were painted white and became very successful cruise liners. During
World War II, VANDYCK became a troopship and was sunk by German
aircraft off Norway in June 1940. At the 1937 Review she was one of five
liners anchored off the head of the lines as a grandstand for Government
guests. The photograph shows her proceeding to her anchorage on the day
before the Review.

87

88

87
P&O SS MOLDAVIA. *Completed:* 1922 16,556 tG. Length: 573ft
beam 71½ft. *Propulsion:* Twin screws: geared turbines: 16 knots. She was
one of the first P&O turbine ships and as built had only one funnel. The second
was added as a 'dummy' (used as a ventilating shaft) during the refit in 1928.
At the Review she was a 'grandstand ship' but was anchored in an outside line
and her passengers could have had but a distant view of the proceedings! She
was broken up in 1938.

88
Blue Star Line SS ARANDORA STAR. *Completed:* 1927 (535×68¼ft)
12,487 tG. *Propulsion:* Twin screws: geared turbines — 8,400 shp: 16
knots. One of five refrigerated passenger and cargo ships built for the
Company's UK-South America service, carrying 350 first class passengers.
In 1929 she completed an extensive refit as a cruise ship and became one of the
best known and best loved of all such pre-WWII ships. At the Naval Review
she was one of the 'grandstands' and was anchored in a very favourable
position to obtain for her passengers an excellent view of the events. During
the war she became a troop transport. She was carrying German and Italian
prisoners when, on 2 July 1940, she was torpedoed and sunk with heavy loss
of life.

89

90

89
The New Zealand Shipping Company's MV RANGITIKI, with four other
liners, was a 'grandstand' for Government guests to the Review and was
anchored off the head of the lines.   The photograph shows her approaching
the area on the day before the Review took place. RANGITIKI sailed between
Southampton or London and Wellington, NZ. She was a comfortable, though
slow ship, with a service speed of 15 knots. She had Sulzer diesels of 10,500
hp, driving twin screws. She was of 16,698 tons gross and was completed in
1929. Her length was 553ft and her beam 70¼ft. During WWII she served as a
troop transport and was broken up in 1962.

90
Seen in this photograph are (L to R) P&O SS COMORIN Blue Star SS
ARANDORA STAR and the Turkish destroyer KOCATEPE.

Coronation Review 1953

The Royal Naval Review at Spithead held on 15 June 1953, was in celebration of the Coronation of Queen Elizabeth II. It will be remembered, not only as a Royal Occasion but also as a very happy event for many of the men and women who had served in the Royal Navy during the Second World War. For this was the first Review of the Fleet since the end of hostilities in 1945 and, although many great ships had been scrapped since then, there was a goodly array of those which had fought so well in the Atlantic, the Pacific and elsewhere.

The character of the Review was greatly changed from that of the last occasion in 1937. Gone were the great battleships, the 'Rs' the 'Queen Elizabeths', NELSON, RODNEY and even the five more recent ships of the 'King George V' Class. In fact, Great Britain had but one battleship, VANGUARD, a beautiful ship armed with 15-inch guns made in 1915 and once fitted to the cruisers COURAGEOUS and GLORIOUS, before they became aircraft carriers.

In 1953, 44 of the 156 naval ships present were frigates and, as one approached the anchorage from Southampton Water, the immediate sight which met the eye was the lines of frigates, most of which had been convoy escorts or support group ships in the Battle of the Atlantic.

Of the 11 British and Commonwealth cruisers present, nine were war veterans, five having served throughout the war. But perhaps the most notable feature of the Review was the great gathering together of aircraft carriers, there being no fewer than nine of these great ships on view. What the battleship had been

to previous Reviews, the carriers were to that of 1953. There were, however, some regrets that all the famous escort carriers and MAC ships were no longer in existence, most of them having been converted back to their merchant status.

In 1953 the Royal Yacht VICTORIA AND ALBERT was but a hulk in Portsmouth Harbour having long since fulfilled her distinguished service and having been an accommodation ship during WW2. Her successor, the Royal Yacht BRITANNIA was still in the hands of the builders. As a result, the Despatch Vessel HMS SURPRISE was used by the Queen to review the Fleet on this occasion. SURPRISE was built as an A/S frigate in 1945, but since the war had been used as the Commander-in-Chief's Yacht in the Mediterranean Fleet. Special sleeping and day cabins were prepared for the Queen and the Duke of Edinburgh and a weatherproof glass and timber reviewing platform was erected in 'B' gun position before the bridge.

There was an impressive display of foreign warships, 16 nations being represented. It was of interest to see Portugal's BARTOLOMEU DIAS again representing her country. She was a new ship in 1935 and was at the Review of 1937. Italy sent her sail training ship AMERIGO VESPUCCI — an elegant and splendid sight with her tall masts. But undoubtedly the ship which engendered most interest was the powerful USSR SVERDLOV, a new ship which was in great contrast with Russia's representative in 1937 — the ancient Battleship MARAT.

In accordance with precedence, SURPRISE was led by the

91
'... as one approached the Review area there were lines of frigates as far as the eye could see...'

Trinity House Yacht PATRICIA and followed by HMS REDPOLE, the Admiralty Yacht. Then came HMS STARLING, FLEETWOOD and HELMSDALE with guests of the Board of Admiralty, C-in-C Portsmouth and the Lord Mayor of Portsmouth with the Mayor of Gosport respectively. Three great liners, ORCADES, PRETORIA CASTLE and STRATHNAVER carrying Government guests followed and the procession ended with the Isle of Wight Passenger Ferries, BRADING and SOUTHSEA carrying Admiralty Staff.

Immediately after the Review came the flypast of aircraft of the Fleet Air Arm. This was a most impressive display, no fewer than 38 Squadrons comprising 300 aircraft flew past the Queen. They were arranged in three formations which passed over SURPRISE at 45-second intervals.

The end of a memorable day came with the illumination of the Fleet at 2230 and a splendid firework display lasting for half-an-hour. At midnight the lights went out and the Review was over.

1953

HM Ship	Type	HM Ship	Type	HM Ship	Type	HM Ship	Type
ACHERON	S/M	FORTH	S.M.D.S.	SANGUINE	S/M	TEREDO	S/M
ADAMANT	S.M.D.S.	GAMBIA	C	SAVAGE	D	TERMAGANT	F
AENEAS	S/M	GLASGOW	C	SCORCHER	S/M	THEMOPYLAE	S/M
AGINCOURT	D	HEDINGHAM CASTLE	F	SCORPION	D	THESEUS	A/C
AISNE	D	HELMSDALE	F	SCOTSMAN	S/M	TINTAGEL CASTLE	F
ALARIC	S/M	ILLUSTRIOUS	A/C	SCOTT	S/S	TIR (IN)	F
ALAUNIA	R/S	IMPLACABLE	A/C	SEA DEVIL	S/M	TIRELESS	S/M
AMBUSH	S/M	INDEFATIGABLE	A/C	SEASCOUT	S/M	TOKEN	S/M
AMPHION	S/M	INDOMITABLE	A/C	SENESCHAL	S/M	TOTEM	S/M
ANCHORITE	S/M	JHELUM (RPN)	F	SENTINEL	S/M	TRADEWIND	S/M
APOLLO	M/LR	JUTLAND	D	SHARPSHOOTER	S/S	TRAFALGAR	D
ARTEMIS	S/M	KNARESBOROUGH		SHEFFIELD	C	TYRIAN	F
ARTFUL	S/M	CASTLE	F	SIDON	S/M	VANGUARD	B/S
ASTUTE	S/M	LAERTES	M/S (O)	SIOUX (RCN)	D	VENUS	F
AURIGA	S/M	LA HULLOISE (RCN)	F	SOLEBAY	D	VERULAM	F
AUROCHS	S/M	LARGO BAY	F	SPRINGER	S/M	VIRAGO	F
BARFLEUR	D	LAUNCESTON CASTLE	F	STARLING	F	WAKEFUL	F
BARROSA	D	LEEDS CASTLE	F	START BAY	F	WELCOME	M/S (O)
BATTLEAXE	D	LOCH RUTHVEN	F	SUPERB	C	WELFARE	M/S (O)
BICESTER	F	LOCH VEYATIE	F	SURPRISE	F	WESSEX (RNVR)	F
BLACK PRINCE (NZ)	C	MAGNIFICENT (RCN)	A/C	SWANSEA (RCN)	F	WIDEMOUTH BAY	F
BOXER	A/D/V	MAGPIE	F	SWIFTSURE	C	WOODBRIDGE HAVEN	F
BRAMBLE	M/S (O)	MAIDSTONE	S.M.D.S.	SYDNEY (RAN)	A/C	WRANGLER	F
BROCKLESBY	F	MANXMAN	M/LR	TALENT	S/M	ZEPHYR	D
BURGHEAD BAY	F	MARVEL	M/S (O)	TALLY HO	S/M	ZULFIQUAR (RPN)	F
CADIZ	D	MELBREAK	F	TENACIOUS	F		
CAISTOR CASTLE	F	MEON	L.S.H.				
CAMPERDOWN	D	MERMAID	F				
CARISBROOK CASTLE	F	MONTCLARE	S.M.D.S.				
CHAMELEON	M/S (O)	MYNGS	D				
CHEERFUL	M/S (O)	OBEDIENT	D				
CLEOPATRA	C	OBDURATE	D	**Foreign Warships**			
CONTEST	D	ONTARIO (RCN)	C				
COOK	S/S	ORCADIA	M/S (O)	Ship	Type	Country	
COQUETTE	M/S (O)	ORWELL	F				
CORUNNA	D	PEACOCK	F	LUITENANT TER ZEE	F	Belgium	
CREOLE	D	PERSEUS	A/C	VICTOR BILLET			
CRISPIN	D	PICKLE	M/S (O)	ALMIRANTE BARROSO	C	Brazil	
CROSSBOW	D	PLOVER	M/S (O)	HOLGER DANSKE	F	Denmark	
CYGNET	F	PLUCKY	M/S (O)	TRUJILLO	D	Dominican Republic	
DECOY	D.C.	PLUTO	M/S (O)	MONTCALM	C	France	
DEFENDER	D.C.	PROTECTOR	N.L.	NAVARINON	D	Greece	
DELHI (IN)	C	QUEBEC (RCN)	C	AMERIGO VESPUCCI	Tr.S	Italy	
DEVONSHIRE	C	RANJIT (IN)	D	TROMP	C	Netherlands	
DIAMOND	D.C.	RATTLESNAKE	M/S (O)	NARVIK	D	Norway	
DIDO	C	REDPOLE	F	BARTOLOMEU DIAS	F	Portugal	
DUCHESS	D.C.	RELENTLESS	F	MIGUEL DE CERVANTES	C	Spain	
EAGLE	A/C	RIFLEMAN	M/S (O)	GOTA LEJON	C	Sweden	
ENARD BAY	F	RINALDO	M/S (O)	POSAMTON	M/S	Thailand	
FIERCE	M/S (O)	ROCKET	F	DEMIRHISAR	D	Turkey	
FINISTERRE	D	ROEBUCK	F	SVERDLOV	C	USSR	
FLEETWOOD	F	ST JAMES	D	BALTIMORE	C	USA	
FLINT CASTLE	F	ST KITTS	D				

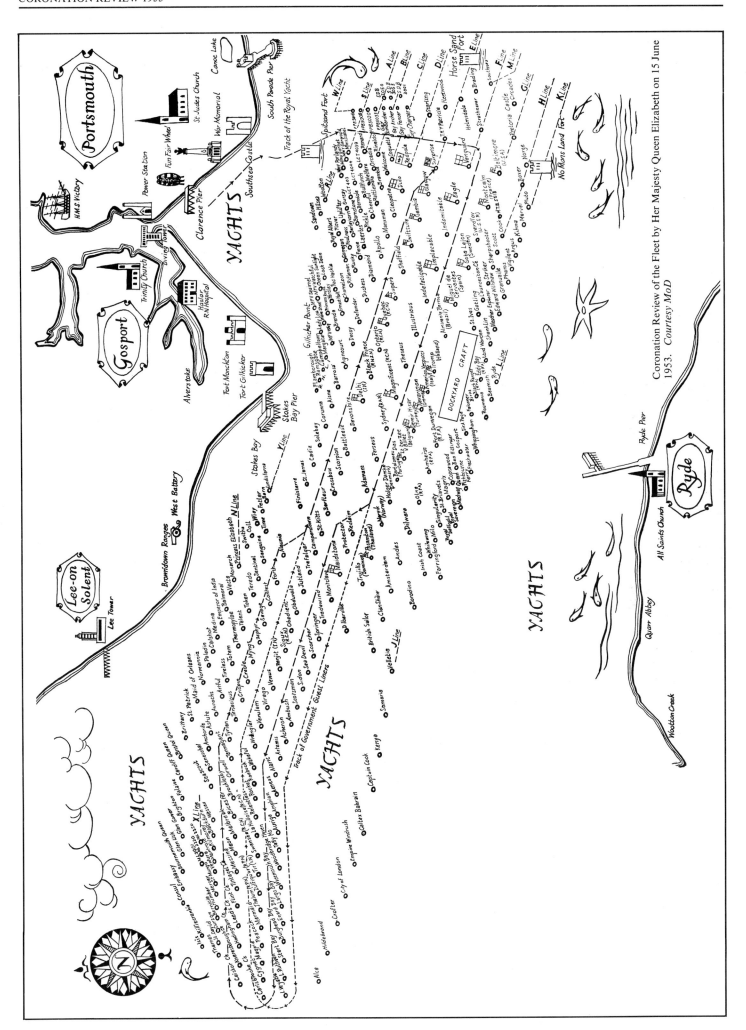

Coronation Review of the Fleet by Her Majesty Queen Elizabeth on 15 June 1953. *Courtesy MoD*

92

93

92

VANGUARD B/S Home Fleet Fleet Flagship. *Completed:* 1946
($814\frac{1}{4} \times 108\frac{1}{2} \times 28$) 44,500/51,420 tD. *Complement:* 1,600 officers and men.
Armament: Eight 15-inch guns in twin turrets. (These guns were not new but
were taken from the Admiralty Armament Reserve. HOOD, the 'Revenge'
Class and the 'Queen Elizabeth' Class battleships used this type of gun.) 16
5.25-inch HA/LA guns in twin turrets formed the secondary armament and
there were 60 Bofors AA guns. *Armour:* 16-inch belt and 15-inch on all
turrets. *Propulsion:* Parsons single-reduction-geared turbines driving two
5-bladed inboard and two 3-bladed outboard propellers: 130,000 shp:
$29\frac{1}{2}$ knots. Eight Admiralty 3-drum boilers with superheaters. VANGUARD
was the largest ever British warship. She saw no war action. She carried the
Royal Family on their highly successful tour of South Africa in 1947, and she
was operational until March 1956 when she was placed in reserve. She was
broken up in 1960. This photograph shows the beautiful lines of her hull.

93

VANGUARD Another view of the great ship, nearly broadside but showing
her square stern.

94

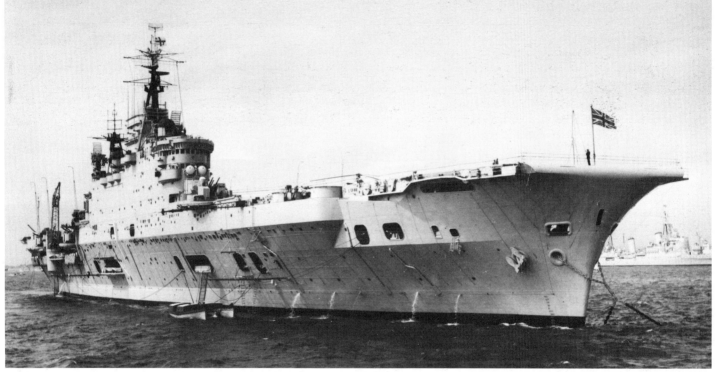

95

94
ILLUSTRIOUS Fleet A/C Home Command, Plymouth. *Completed:*
1940. Dimensions and details as for INDOMITABLE which, however, had a
slightly larger hangar (Plate 98). ILLUSTRIOUS had a particularly busy time
during WWII serving in the Home Fleet (Norwegian Campaign), in the
Mediterranean (Taranto, Malta convoys), the Madagascar Campaign and later
in the Far East. She was badly damaged by bombing in 1941 but was repaired
in the United States. This gallant old ship was broken up in 1956.

95
EAGLE A/C Flagship, Heavy Squadron, Home Fleet. *Completed:* 1951
(803×112×33¼) 43,060/53,000 tD. *Complement:* 1,425 officers and men
including flying personnel. *Armament:* 16 4.5-inch HA/LA and 62 smaller
AA guns. *Propulsion:* Quadruple screws — Parsons single-reduction-geared
turbines: 152,000 shp: 31½ knots. Largest aircraft carrier in the Royal Navy
— ARK ROYAL was a sister ship completed in 1955. Her hull was almost
completely of welded construction. EAGLE was the first carrier to operate jet
aircraft. Her hangar could accommodate up to 110 aircraft according to type.
Two large aircraft lifts. She was exceptionally well sub-divided but, at the same
time, had excellent accommodation for her crew. During 1959-64 she was
reconstructed with angled flight deck and with protection against nuclear
fall-out. She was broken up in 1978.

96

97

96
IMPLACABLE A/C Home Fleet. *Completed:* 1944. $(766\frac{1}{4} \times 95\frac{3}{4} \times 29\frac{1}{2})$
23,000/32,060 tD. *Complement:* About 1,785 officers and men including air
personnel. *Armament:* 16 4.5-inch HA/LA in twin mountings: 80 smaller AA
guns. Carried 72 aircraft. *Armour:* $4\frac{1}{2}$-inch belts; 3-inch deck. *Propulsion:*
Quadruple screws driven by Parsons single-reduction-geared turbines: 148,000
shp: 32 knots. Her sister ship was INDEFATIGABLE, completed three
months earlier. IMPLACABLE carried out a number of strikes on the
Norwegian coast and in the last quarter of 1944, her aircraft sank or damaged
68,700 tons of German shipping and they found the Battleship TIRPITZ in
Trömso Fjord, where the RAF later sank her. She went to the Pacific in 1945,
attacking the Caroline Islands and then her aircraft operated against Japan
and sank over 150,000 tons of enemy shipping. She was broken up in 1955.

97
INDEFATIGABLE A/C Home Fleet. *Completed:* 1944. Dimensions
and details as for IMPLACABLE (Plate 96). During WWII she first served
with the Home Fleet and her aircraft took part in two abortive attacks on the
TIRPITZ in 1944. In November of the same year INDEFATIGABLE was
one of five fleet carriers assembled at Trincomalee for the formation of the
British Pacific Fleet, and, at the end of the year she took part in a successful
raid on an oil refinery in Sumatra. She was involved with the operations
against Ishigaki and Miyako with three other carriers and a number of cruisers
including SWIFTSURE and GAMBIA (qv). During the attacks on Okinawa
in April 1945 INDEFATIGABLE was hit by a Japanese suicide bomber but
she was saved from serious damage by her 3-inch armoured flight deck. She
was broken up in 1956.

98

INDOMITABLE A/C Home Fleet. *Completed:* 1941. (754×95×22½)
23,000/29,730 tD. *Complement:* 1,600 officers and men including flying
personnel. *Armament:* 16 4.5-inch HA/LA guns, 48 2-pdr pompoms and
many smaller AA guns. *Armour:* 4½-inch belts and hangar sides. 3-inch flight
deck. *Propulsion:* Triple screws powered by Parsons single-reduction-geared
turbines: 110,000 shp: 31 knots. She carried 72 aircraft. During WW2
INDOMITABLE was first working in the Far East and in the Madagascar
Campaign. In August 1942, while part of Force H at Gibraltar, she took part
in the heavily protected convoy to Malta code-named 'Pedestal' but
remembered mainly for the heroic and successful effort of the tanker OHIO
which, though terribly damaged, got her cargo of aviation spirit through to
Malta. INDOMITABLE had her flight deck severely damaged by bombs and
her aircraft had to land on VICTORIOUS. After being repaired,
INDOMITABLE spent the rest of the war with the Eastern Fleet and on
operations in the Pacific. She was scrapped in 1955.

99

THESEUS 'Colossus' Class Light Fleet Aircraft Carrier. Home Fleet.
Completed: 1946 (695×112½×21¼) 13,350 tD. *Complement:* 1,076
officers and men including air personnel. *Armament:* 18 Bofors AA guns and
24 2-pdr pompoms. *Armour:* 1-inch deck. *Propulsion:* Twin screws (one
three-bladed and one four-bladed) driven by Parsons single-reduction-geared
turbines: 40,000 shp: 25 knots. Four Admiralty 3-drum boilers with
superheaters providing superheated steam at 400 psi and 700°F. She went
into service only a short time before the end of WWII but gave valuable
assistance in the Korean War. She was broken up in 1962.

100

PERSEUS (ex EDGAR) Aircraft Maintenance Ship Home Command,
Portsmouth. *Completed:* 1945 (695×80¼×18¼) 12,265/16,475 tD.
Complement: 1,076 officers and men. *Armament:* 12 2-pdr pompoms and 10
smaller AA guns. *Propulsion:* Parsons single-reduction-geared turbines
driving twin screws: 42,000 shp: 25 knots. Her service during WWII was
with the Pacific Fleet. In 1951 she was refitted and provided with a steam
catapult. She was then designated 'Ferry Carrier'. At the Review she was a
'grandstand' for official guests and had banks of seats erected on her flight
deck. The photograph shows the British Railways MV BRADING alongside
with guests transhipping to the carrier. PERSEUS was broken up in 1958.

101

102

101
GLASGOW C Fleet Flagship Mediterranean Fleet. *Completed:* 1937
($591\frac{1}{2} \times 61\frac{3}{4} \times 17$) 9,100/12,400 tD. *Complement:* 825 officers and men.
Armament: Nine 6-inch guns in triple turrets, eight 4-inch AA, 24 2-pdr
pompoms and eight smaller guns. Six 21-inch torpedo tubes. *Armour:* 4-inch
belts and conning tower; 2-inch turrets. *Propulsion:* Quadruple screws driven
by Parsons single-reduction-geared turbines: 75,000 shp: 32 knots.
GLASGOW was the fourth ship of the 'Southampton' Class (Plate 54) and
originally carried three aircraft in a hangar abaft the bridge and had a catapult
between the funnels. She also had 12 6-inch guns but the three in X turret were
removed and replaced by eight Bofors AA guns. She had a distinguished
career during WWII and evacuated the King, the Crown Prince and
Government of Norway from Molde, later transferring them to
DEVONSHIRE at Aandalsnes. At the end of 1940 she went to the Eastern
Mediterranean but later returned to the Home Fleet to land Royal Marines in
Iceland in response to a German threat. 1943 was a good year for the
GLASGOW for she intercepted the REGENSBURG, a German supply ship,
and later the same year, intercepted another supply ship escorted by four
destroyers. GLASGOW in company with ENTERPRISE sank three of the
destroyers and the supply ship. At the Review, GLASGOW was commanded
by a famous submariner, Captain 'Bill' Bryant while she wore the Flag of
Admiral the Earl Mountbatten of Burma who was Commander-in-Chief
Mediterranean Fleet. She was broken up in 1958.

102
SUPERB C America and West Indies Station. *Completed:* 1945
($555\frac{1}{2} \times 64 \times 16\frac{1}{2}$) 9,000/11,560 tD. *Complement:* 867 officers and men.
Armament: Nine 6-inch guns in triple turrets, 10 4-inch AA and 36 smaller
AA guns. Eight 21-inch torpedo tubes. *Armour:* 4-inch belt; 2-inch turrets
and deck. *Propulsion:* Quadruple screws: Parsons single-reduction-geared
turbines: 72,500 shp. $31\frac{1}{2}$ knots. She was completed too late in WWII to be
able to take part in any major operation. SUPERB was broken up in 1960

103

104

105

103

SWIFTSURE C Flagship (Flotillas) Home Fleet. *Completed:* 1944
Dimensions and details as for SUPERB (Plate 102) except: 8,800/11,240 tD.
Complement: 855 officers and men. *Armament:* Nine 6-inch guns in triple
turrets. 12 4-inch, eight Bofors and 24 smaller AA guns. SWIFTSURE was
in the British Pacific Fleet and was at the capture of the Sakishima Gunto
group of islands and also was the Flagship of Rear-Admiral Harcourt at the
re-occupation of Hong Kong. She was for disposal in 1962.

104

GAMBIA C Flagship (Flotillas) Mediterranean Fleet. *Completed:* 1942
$(555\frac{1}{2} \times 62 \times 16\frac{1}{2})$ 8,000/11,270 tD. *Complement:* 750 officers and men.
Armament: Nine 6-inch in triple turrets, eight 4-inch AA, 12 40mm AA guns.
Six 21-inch torpedo tubes. *Armour:* $4\frac{1}{2}$-inch belt. 4-inch conning tower. 2-inch
turrets and deck. *Propulsion:* Quadruple screws: Parsons single-reduction-
geared turbines: 72,500 shp: $31\frac{1}{2}$ knots. One of the 'Colony' class cruisers —
a development of the 'Southampton' Class with vertical funnels and masts. The
original design included 12 6-inch guns but 'X' turret was removed in those so
built and the last three were built with only nine 6-inch guns, the space
occupied by 'X' turret being given over to anti-aircraft guns. GAMBIA was
lent to the RNZN in 1943 but returned to RN in 1946. She spent most of her
time during WWII in the Far East and was involved in operations with the US
Fleet, including the attack on Sabang in April 1944 and later, attacks on the
islands of Ishigaki and Miyako. She was broken up in 1968.

105

DIDO C Fleet Flagship, Reserve Fleet. *Completed:* 1940 ($512 \times 50\frac{1}{2} \times 14$)
5,770/7,400 tD. *Complement:* 551 officers and men. *Armament:* 10 5.25
HA/LA in twin turrets, eight 2-pdr pompom and 16 smaller guns. When built
she had but four turrets, a 3-inch gun being in 'C' position. The fifth turret was
fitted in 1941 at Brooklyn Navy Yard. Six 21-inch torpedo tubes. *Armour:*
2-inch belt and turrets. *Propulsion:* Quadruple screws powered by Parsons
single-reduction-geared turbines: 64,000 shp: $32\frac{1}{4}$ knots. Joined the Home
Fleet and made a number of patrols to the Denmark Strait. Also acted as anti-
aircraft escort for fast convoys to West Coast of Africa and in the Atlantic. In
1941, joined the Mediterranean Fleet in company with ABDIEL and six
destroyers. Escort to Malta convoys and was very active during the Crete
campaign. During the final evacuation she was badly damaged by a 1,000lb
bomb from a Stuka. Repaired in USA and returned to the Mediterranean in
early 1942. Was in Force K. Was in the Battle of Sirte and again did good
work on Malta convoys. Later she gave excellent gunnery support at the Anzio
beachhead. Finally, she was present at the German surrender at Copenhagen.
At the Review, she wore the flag of Rear Admiral H. W. U. McCall, KBE, CB,
DSO, who was her Captain during her first commission. DIDO was broken up
in 1958

106
DIDO and CLEOPATRA Anti-aircraft cruisers and sister ships were both in
the Reserve Fleet (DIDO being the Flagship). Details and description of
DIDO will be found under Plate 105. CLEOPATRA was broken up in 1958.

107

108

109

107
MANXMAN   Fast Minelayer   Mediterranean Fleet.   *Completed:* 1941
(410×39×11¼)   2,650/4,000 tD.   *Complement:* 246 officers and men.
Armament: Four 4-inch HA/LA guns in twin mounts forward of the bridge.
Six Bofors AA. Carried 108 mines.   *Propulsion:* Twin screws driven by
Parsons single-reduction-geared turbines: 72,000 shp: 40 knots. Four
Admiralty 3-drum boilers with superheaters.   Originally four ships in the
class, ABDIEL, LATONA, and WELSHMAN being the other three which
were WWII casualties. APOLLO and ARIADNE were later ships of the same
class. With their high speed, these ships were most useful, not only laying
mines but acting as cruisers in Mediterranean convoys, running stores to
Malta and troops to Alexandria. MANXMAN served for a time in the Eastern
Fleet but ended her war service in the Home Fleet. After the war she became a
support ship for minesweepers. She was broken up in 1972.

108
BATTLEAXE   D 'Weapon' Class   Home Fleet.   *Completed:* 1947
(365×38×12½ (max))   2,000/2,840 tD.   *Complement:* 265.   *Armament:* Four

4-inch in twin mounts, six small AA guns. 10 21-inch torpedo tubes in
quintuple mountings. *A/S Weapons:* Two Squid 3-barrelled throwers.
Propulsion: Twin screws driven by Parsons single-reduction-geared turbines:
40,000 shp: 34½ knots. Two boilers with superheaters providing steam at
430 psi at 750°F. Each boiler and each set of turbines had its own
compartment resulting in two widely spaced funnels, the foremost of which is
'enclosed' in the single lattice mast.   These four ships were designed as Fleet
A/S Escorts. BATTLEAXE was broken up in 1964.

109
SCORPION   D 'Weapon' Class Destroyer   Home Fleet.   *Completed:*
1947.   Description and details as for BATTLEAXE (Plate 108) except that
SCORPION had Limbo 3-barrelled depth charge mortar in place of two
Squids. This view clearly shows the foremost funnel 'enclosed' by the lattice
mast. SCORPION was first named CENTAUR and then TOMAHAWK. She
was broken up in 1971.

110

111

110
DECOY 'Daring' Class ship Fleet Escort. *Completed:* 1953, only a month before appearing at the Review. (390×43×12¾). *Complement:* 295 officers and men. *Armament:* Six 4.5-inch HA/LA guns in twin turrets. Six Bofors AA guns. 10 21-inch torpedo tubes in quintuple mounts. *A/S armament:* One Squid 3-barrelled thrower. *Propulsion:* PAMETRADA double-reduction-geared turbines driving twin screws: 54,000 shp: 34½ knots. The disposition of the two boilers and turbines is the same as that for BATTLEAXE (Plate 108). At the time of their introduction the 'Daring Class Ships' were the largest destroyers ever built for the Royal Navy and among the first to have completely welded hulls. DECOY was originally named DRAGON. She was sold to Peru in 1970.

111
FINISTERRE D 'First Battle' Class Destroyer Portsmouth Command Home Fleet. *Completed:* 1945. This ship and her sister were intended for service in the Pacific but the war ended before they could be deployed. (379×40¼×12¾). 2,315 tD. *Complement:* 275 officers and men. *Armament:* Four 4.5-inch in twin turrets forward of the bridge: nine smaller AA guns. Two depth charge throwers Eight 21-inch torpedo tubes. *Propulsion:* Twin screws driven by Parsons single-reduction-geared turbines: 50,000 shp: 35¾ knots. FINISTERRE was broken up in 1966.

112

113

112
AISNE D Second 'Battle' Class Fleet Destroyer Home Fleet. *Completed:*
1947 (379×40¼×12¾) 2,460 tD. *Complement:* 232 officers and men.
Armament: Five 4.5-inch and eight 40mm AA guns. 10 21-inch torpedo tubes
in two mounts. *A/S Weapons:* One Squid 3-barrelled depth charge mortar.
Propulsion: Twin screws driven by Parsons single-reduction-geared turbines:
50,000 shp: 35¾ knots. In 1962 she was converted to a Fleet Radar Picket,
little of the original ship being left. She then also carried a Seacat (surface to
air) guided missile launcher. She was broken up in 1970.

113
OBEDIENT D 'Onslow' Class Nore Command. *Completed:* 1942
(345×35×9) 1,900/2,420 tD. *Complement:* 175 officers and men.
Armament: Four 4-inch guns in single mountings. 12 smaller guns including
eight AA. Eight 21-inch torpedo tubes. *Propulsion:* Parsons single-reduction-
geared turbines: twin screws: 40,000 shp: 34 knots. Fitted as minelayer.
OBEDIENT played a valiant part in the defence of the Russian convoy JW 51
B when the convoy was attacked by the German cruiser HIPPER and three
destroyers on 31 December 1942. Later, in 1943, she joined the 3rd Escort
Group, one of the famous five Atlantic Support Groups. She was broken up in
1962.

114

115

116

117

118

114
ORWELL Fast Anti-Submarine Frigate (limited conversion from Destroyer) Home Command, Scotland. *Completed:* 1942 *Converted:* 1952 (345×35×9) 1,800/2,300 tD. *Complement:* 175 officers and men. *Armament:* Two 4-inch HA/LA guns in a twin mount, forward of the bridge. Two 40mm Bofors AA aft. Four 21-inch torpedo tubes. *A/S Weapons:* Two Squid 3-barrelled depth charge mortars. *Propulsion:* Parsons single-reduction-geared turbines: 40,000 shp: 34 knots. ORWELL was a sister ship to OBEDIENT which was not converted to Frigate. Both ships were fitted as minelayers. During WWII with OBEDIENT and other ships, ORWELL took part in the defence of Russian convoy JW 51 B when it was attacked by the HIPPER and later formed part of the 3rd Escort Group. (Plate 113)

115
TERMAGANT Fast Anti-Submarine Frigate (limited conversion from Destroyer) Home Command, Plymouth. *Completed:* 1943 *Converted:* 1952 (362¾×35½×10) 1,730/2,530 tD. *Complement:* 180 officers and men. *Armament:* Two 4-inch HA/LA guns in a single mount forward of the bridge. Seven Bofors AA. Torpedo tubes removed. *A/S Weapons:* Two Squid 3-barrelled depth charge mortars. *Propulsion:* Twin screws: Parsons single-reduction-geared turbines: 40,000 shp: 36¾ knots. During WWII TERMAGANT served latterly with the Mediterranean Fleet and, with TUSCAN, sank two Italian destroyers, then manned by the Germans, during the German evacuation of Crete in October, 1944. She was broken up in 1965.

116
WRANGLER Fast Anti-Submarine Frigate — (full conversion from Destroyer). *Completed:* 1944 *Converted:* 1951-52 (362¾×35¾×11) 2,100/2,700 tD. *Complement:* 175 officers and men. *Armament:* Two 4-inch guns and two Bofors AA. *A/S Weapons:* Two Squid 3-barrelled depth charge mortars. *Propulsion:* Parsons single-reduction-geared turbines driving twin screws: 40,000 shp: 36¾ knots. In 1957 WRANGLER was sold to South Africa and became SAN VRYSTART. She was sunk as a target in 1976.

117
MELBREAK 'Hunt' Class Frigate originally Type 3 'Hunt' Class Destroyer. *Completed:* 1942 (280×31½×7¾) 1,050/1,490 tD. *Complement:* 168 officers and men. *Armament:* Four 4-inch HA/LA, one 4-barrelled pompom, 3 smaller AA guns. Two 21-inch torpedo tubes. *Propulsion:* Twin screws: Parsons single-reduction-geared turbines 19,000 shp: 25 knots. Two Admiralty 3-drum boilers. During WWII MELBREAK and her sisters were used mainly as anti-aircraft convoy escorts in the English Channel and the North Sea. Their losses were heavy. After the war several were sold to foreign navies. Seen behind MELBREAK in the photograph are, left to right, ROCKET, MAINE (hospital ship) and RELENTLESS. MELBREAK was broken up in 1956.

118
MERMAID A/S Frigate, formerly modified 'Black Swan' Class Sloop, Mediterranean Fleet *Completed:* 1944. Description and details as for MAGPIE (Plate 119). During the last months of WWII the ship was engaged in convoy escort duties in the North Atlantic. In 1958 she was sold to West Germany and was renamed SCHARNHORST, being employed for gunnery training.

119

120

119
MAGPIE A/S Frigate, formerly modified 'Black Swan' Class Sloop
Mediterranean Fleet. *Completed:* 1943 (299½×38×8¾) 1,490/1,975 tD.
Complement: 192 officers and men. *Armament:* Six 4-inch and eight smaller
AA guns. *A/S Weapons:* One Hedgehog, four depth charge throwers.
Propulsion: Parsons single-reduction-geared turbines driving twin screws:
4,300 shp: 20 knots designed speed. She was, however, fitted with stabilisers
and extra Asdic equipment to locate deep-dived submarines. These, and other
items of extra equipment, increased her standard displacement from 1,350 to
1,490 tons and reduced her speed to about 16 knots. During WWII MAGPIE
was a member of Captain F. J. Walker's 2nd Support (escort) Group which
was so very successful against the German U-boats in the North Atlantic.
After the war, from 1949 to 1951 MAGPIE was commanded by Lieutenant-
Commander Prince Philip, Duke of Edinburgh. She was broken up in 1959.

120
LEEDS CASTLE A/S Frigate (formerly Corvette) Home Command,
Portsmouth. *Completed:* 1944 (301¼×36½×9) 1,100/1,580 tD.
Complement: 120 officers and men. *Armament:* One 4-inch and 10 20mm
AA guns (In fact, very few of the class had their full armament as AA guns
were in 'short supply'. Most of the 'Castles' had only six 20mm AA and a few
only four). *A/S Weapons:* One Squid depth charge mortar. *Propulsion:*
Single screw driven by one 4-cylinder triple expansion engine: 2,880 ihp:
16 knots. The 20 'Castle Class Corvettes' were all completed between
October 1943 and January 1945 after the Battle of the Atlantic had passed its
peak. They were a development of the famous 'Flower' Class which did such
great service during the height of the battle. LEEDS CASTLE was broken up
in 1958

121
LARGO BAY (ex LOCH FIONN) 'Bay' Class Frigate Home Command,
Scotland. *Completed:* 1946 1,600 tD. *Complement:* 157 officers and men.
Armament: Four 4-inch and 10 small AA guns. *A/S Weapons:* Two
Hedgehogs, (ahead thrown weapons). *Propulsion:* Twin screws driven by two
4-cylinder triple expansion engines: 5,500 ihp: 19½ knots. Two Admiralty
3-drum W.T. boilers. Some ships of much the same design carried the names
of 'Lochs' and several changed their names. There were some differences
between the two designs and generally. the 'Bays' had a greater displacement
by 170 tons. Two of the 'Lochs' were driven by geared turbines which gave
them a speed of 20 knots. LARGO BAY was broken up in 1958.

122
LOCH RUTHVEN A/S Escort Frigate Home Command, Plymouth.
Completed: 1945 (307×38½×12) 1,575/2,400 tD. *Complement:* 130
officers and men. *A/S Weapons:* Two Squid 3-barrelled depth charge mortars. *Propulsion:* Twin
screws driven by two triple expansion engines: 5,500 ihp: 19½ knots. LOCH
RUTHVEN and most of her sisters were refitted and given an extra 4-inch gun
and two extra Bofors. (Originally only one 4-inch and four Bofors). The
'Lochs' were excellent sea-boats and a development of the 'River' Class
corvettes (later called frigates). LOCH RUTHVEN was for disposal in 1963.

123
SURPRISE ex GERRANS BAY ex LOCH CARRON Originally designed
as a 'Loch' Class Frigate but completed as a despatch vessel or 'C-in-C's
Yacht' In the 1953 Review she acted as the Reviewing Ship or deputy Royal
Yacht as VICTORIA AND ALBERT was no more than a hulk and
BRITANNIA had not yet been completed. The twin 4-inch guns in 'B'
position were removed and a glass-enclosed platform or dais erected for Her
Majesty and Prince Philip. The photograph shows the ship at Portsmouth on
the day preceding the Review. Specification as for LOCH RUTHVEN qv
(Plate 122). She was broken up in 1970.

121

122

123

124

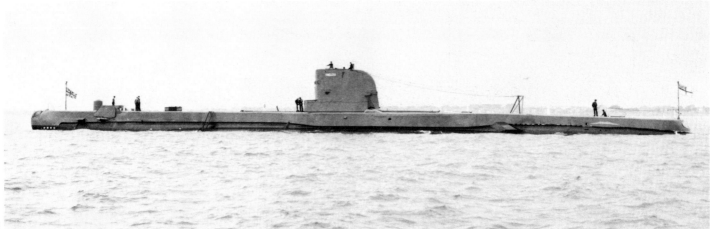

125

126

Three 'T' Class Patrol Submarines

124

TOKEN (Mediterranean Fleet). *Completed:* 1945. Shown as built
($273\frac{1}{2}\times26\frac{1}{2}\times14\frac{3}{4}$) 1,231/1,575 tD. *Complement:* 6 officers and 59 ratings.
Armament: One 4-inch gun; 11 21-inch torpedo tubes. *Propulsion:* Twin
screw: Diesel motors (surface): $15\frac{1}{2}$ knots. Electric motors (submerged):
9 knots. She was broken up in 1965.

125

TIRELESS (Submarine Command). *Completed:* 1945. Riveted hull.
Partially rebuilt and streamlined 1953. *Armament:* Six 21-inch torpedo tubes
(carried 17 torpedoes). *Propulsion:* Twin screw, Diesel and electric. Fitted
with Schnorkel. Submerged speed 15 knots. Broken up 1968.

126

THERMOPYLAE (Submarine Command). *Completed:* 1945. Welded
hull. Rebuilt and lengthened by 20ft. 1,505/1,700 tD. *Armament:* Six
21-inch torpedo tubes (carried 17 torpedoes). *Propulsion:* Twin screw Diesel
and electric. Fitted with Schnorkel. Submerged speed: 15 knots. Broken up
1970.

127

128

127

MONTCLARE Depot Ship — Submarines. Completed as a Canadian Pacific liner in 1922. Twin screw. Direct drive turbines, 16 knots. (550×70×28) 16,314 tG. Re-engined with single-reduction-geared turbines in 1929, 12,500 shp: 17 knots. On the outbreak of WWII she was requisitioned as an Armed Merchant Cruiser but, in 1942, was sold to Admiralty for conversion to a Submarine Depot Ship. She became Flagship to the fleet train (supply) in the Pacific but later was parent ship to the submarine flotillas at Rothesay. As HMS MONTCLARE she was of 21,550 tD and was armed with four 4-inch HA/LA and 32 2-pdr AA guns. Her complement was 480 officers and men. MONTCLARE was broken up in 1958.

128

ALAUNIA Heavy Repair Ship, Home Command, Plymouth *Completed:* 1925. The last of six Cunard 'A' Class ships built between 1922 and 1925 for service between United Kingdom and Canada. ALAUNIA was of 14,030 tG a twin screw ship driven by double-reduction-geared turbines and with a speed of 15 knots. At the outbreak of WWII five of the six ships became Armed Merchant Cruisers but three, AUSONIA, ALAUNIA and AURANIA were later converted to Fleet Repair Ships, AURANIA became HMS ARTIFEX, the other two retained their original names. HMS ALAUNIA (538×65¼×31½) was of 19,000 tD and was armed with 20 20mm AA guns. She spent much of the war in the East Indies but, afterwards, was based at Devonport as a training ship for engine-room ratings. She was broken up in 1957.

129

130

129

ADAMANT Depot Ship — Submarines Reserve Fleet. *Completed:* 1942 (658×70½×20) 12,700/16,500 tD. *Complement:* 1,273 officers and men (includes accommodation for crews of one submarine flotilla). *Armament:* Eight 4.5-inch HA/LA in twin mounts and 36 smaller AA guns. *Propulsion:* Twin screws driven by Parsons single-reduction-geared turbines: 8,000 shp: 17 knots. She was Depot Ship Submarines Eastern Fleet until 1944 when she went to the Pacific Fleet. Broken up in 1970.

130

MAIDSTONE Depot Ship, Submarines and Flagship Submarine Command. *Completed:* 1938 (531×73×20) 8,900 tD. *Complement:* 502 officers and men of whom 43 were spare submarine crew and 64 were repair staff. *Armament:* Eight 4.5-inch and 10 smaller AA guns. *Propulsion:* Brown-Curtis single-reduction-geared turbines driving twin screws: 7,000 shp: 17 knots. Sister ship was FORTH. MAIDSTONE was based at Alexandria for most of WWII but in 1944 she moved to Western Australia. She ended her days as an accommodation ship for the Army in Belfast and was used to lodge IRA prisoners. She was broken up in 1978.

131

132

131
CHAMELEON 'Algerine' Class Ocean Minesweeper Mediterranean
Fleet. *Completed:* 1944 (235×35½×10) 850/1,050 tD. *Complement:* 85.
Armament: One 4-inch gun, four Bofors AA. *A/S Weapons:* Four depth
charge throwers. *Propulsion:* Twin screws driven by single-reduction-geared
turbines: 2,000 shp: 16½ knots. This was one of 112 'Algerines' of which 30
had turbines and the rest two triple expansion engines. The ships were often
used as A/S escorts but having a shallow draught were very lively in anything
but a calm sea. CHAMELEON was broken up in 1966.

132
RECLAIM (ex SALVERDANT) Deep Diving and Submarine Rescue
Vessel based on the 'King Salvor' Class of salvage vessels but modified during
construction. *Completed:* 1948 (217×38×15) 1,200/1,800 tD.
Complement: 84 officers and men. *Propulsion:* Twin screws driven by two
triple expansion engines: 1,500 ihp: 12 knots. She was the first ship of her
type to be built for the Royal Navy. During her career she was an experimental
deep diving ship, a mine counter-measure support ship and a diving trials ship.
For her duties she was equipped with Asdic, echo-sounding and radar. She had
the distinction of being the only RN ship to be present at both the 1953 and the
1977 Royal Naval Reviews. She was for disposal 1981.

133

134

133
BRENDA   Patrol Ship, Fishery Board for Scotland.   *Completed:* 1951
$(178\frac{3}{4}\times26\times10\frac{1}{4})$ 350 tG.   *Propulsion:* Twin screws. Two 7-cylinder Polar
diesels: 14 knots.   Still in service.

134
ERNEST HOLT   Ministry of Agriculture and Fisheries   Research trawler.
Completed: 1948 $(177\frac{1}{2}\times30\frac{1}{4}\times17\frac{1}{2})$ 604 tG.   *Propulsion:* Single screw,
3-cylinder triple expansion engine.   In 1971 she was renamed SWITHA on
becoming a Fisheries Protection and Surveillance ship for the Department of
Agriculture and Fisheries for Scotland. Her gross tonnage then was 573. On
31 January 1950, during a gale she went aground on the island of Inchkeith in
the Firth of Forth and became a constructive total loss. Her crew were taken
off by helicopter and the wreck was later blown up.

135

136

135
RANJIT D Indian Navy ex RN Fleet Destroyer, REDOUBT.
Completed: 1942 (358¼×35½×9½) 1,735/2,495 tD. *Complement:* 200 officers and men. *Armament:* Four 4.7-inch guns in single mountings; four 40mm AA; two 2-pdr AA. Eight 21-inch torpedo tubes. Four depth charge throwers. *Propulsion:* Parsons single-reduction-geared turbines: twin screws: 43,000 shp: 34 knots. RANJIT was one of three R Class destroyers transferred to India early in 1950. The R Class ships were of interest in that they were the first British destroyers in which the officers' accommodation was placed forward instead of aft. Broken up in 1979.

136
ZULFIQUAR (ex DHANUSH (RIN) '48 ex DEVERON '45) Royal Pakistan Navy. *Completed:* as 'River' Class Corvette (Frigate) in 1943. (301½×36½×12) 1,370/2,100 tD. *Complement:* 140 officers and men. *Armament:* Two 4-inch, 10 20mm AA guns. (Probably only six were fitted). *A/S Weapons:* One Hedgehog ATW. *Propulsion:* Twin screws (inward turning) powered by two 4-cylinder triple expansion engines: 5,500 ihp: 20 knots. ZULFIQUAR was converted to a Surveying Ship in 1955.

137

138

137
BLACK PRINCE   C   Later 'Dido' Class   Royal New Zealand Navy.
Completed: 1943   (512×50½×15)   5,900/7,410 tD.   *Complement:* 550
officers and men.   *Armament:* Eight 5.25-inch HA/LA; four 40mm, 12 2-pdr
and three 20mm guns, all AA. Four 3-pdr Saluting guns. Six 21-inch torpedo
tubes.   *Armour:* 2-inch belts and 1-inch turrets. *Propulsion:* Quadruple screws
driven by Parsons single-reduction-geared turbines: 64,000 shp: 32 knots.
BLACK PRINCE was one of four ships which differed from the 'Dido' Class
in having vertical funnels and masts and eight 5.25 guns instead of 10. She was
given to the New Zealand Navy in 1948 and was broken up in 1962. BLACK
PRINCE had a short but effective record during WWII. In February 1944 she
was Flagship of the escort to a large convoy bound for the Kola Inlet in Russia
and in April the same year she was in action against German torpedo boats in
the Channel. Three months later she was accurately bombarding German gun
positions on the Normandy coast. In November 1944 she joined what was to
become the British Pacific Fleet at Trincomalee, Ceylon. In April 1945 she
played an active part with the fleet which captured the island of Okinawa.

138
MAGNIFICENT   Royal Canadian Navy (on loan)   Light Fleet Aircraft
Carrier.   *Completed:* 1948   (698×112×25)   15,700/19,550 tD.
Complement: 1,350 officers and men including air personnel.   *Armament:*
Four 3-pdr. 30 40mm Bofors AA guns.   *Aircraft:* 34-48 according to type.
Propulsion: Twin screws driven by Parsons single-reduction-geared turbines.
Four Admiralty 3-drum boilers. The boiler and engine rooms were staggered,
the port side power unit being further forward than that of the starboard side.
MAGNIFICENT was returned to the Royal Navy in 1957. She was broken
up in 1965.

139
SWANSEA and LA HULLOISE. Canada Canadian-built Frigates. *Completed:* 1942 and 1943 respectively. Follow closely the design of the British 'River' Class. 1,445 tD. *Complement:* 140 officers and men. *Armament:* Two 4-inch and 10 20mm AA guns. *A/S Weapons:* Two 'Hedgehog' and two depth charge throwers. *Propulsion:* Twin (inward turning) screws driven by triple expansion engines: 5,500 ihp: 20 knots. These ships spent most of WWII on North Atlantic escort duties. They were excellent sea boats. Later, the two with their twelve sisters, were modernised, re-armed and converted to flush deckers.

140
D'IBERVILLE Government of Canada (MOT) Icebreaker *Completed:* 1953 5,678 tG. Steamship Twin screw. Two Uniflow 6-cylinder engines, each of 6,000 shp driving twin screws. Accommodation for 12 passengers. This interesting ship was probably the newest at the Review having been completed only in May, 1953.

141

142

143

141
HOLGER DANSKE Denmark Frigate Ex HMS MONNOW.
Completed: 1944 (301¼×36½×12) 1,452 tD. *Complement:* 140 officers and
men. *Armament:* Two 5-inch AA and eleven smaller AA guns. Two 18-inch
torpedo tubes. *Propulsion:* Two 4-cylinder triple expansion engines driving
twin screws. 6,500 ihp: 20 knots. As MONNOW during WWII she was on
North Atlantic convoy escort duties and worked with a Canadian group. She
was, in 1953, a training ship for midshipmen.

142
NARVIK Norway Frigate ex HMS GLAISDALE 'Hunt' Class Type 2
Destroyer (later Frigate). *Completed:* 1942 (280×31½×7¾) 1,050/
1,490 tD. *Complement:* 202 officers and men. *Armament:* Four 4-inch AA,
and 6 smaller AA guns. Two 21-inch torpedo tubes. *A/S Weapons:* two
depth charge throwers. *Propulsion:* Twin screws — Parsons single-reduction-
geared turbines: 19,000 shp: 25 knots. NARVIK was broken up in Denmark
in 1961.

143
NAVARINON Greece D ex HMS ECHO qv (Plate 34). She was loaned
to the Royal Hellenic Navy in 1944 and, after WWII became a training ship.
She was broken up in 1956.

144

145

144
DEMIRHISAR Turkey D. *Completed:* 1942 (323×33×8½) 1,360/
2,100 tD. *Complement:* 150 officers and men. *Armament:* Four 4.7-inch and
eight smaller AA guns. Eight 21-inch torpedo tubes. *Propulsion:* Twin screws
driven by Parsons single-reduction-geared turbines: 34,000 shp: 33 knots.
Three 3-drum boilers with WP 300 psi. She was one of three ships, almost
identical with the British 'I' Class destroyers, completed during WWII in
British yards. Two were delivered to Turkey but one was commandeered by
the Royal Navy as HMS INCONSTANT and returned to Turkey in 1945 as
their MUAVENET.

145
TROMP Netherlands L/C. *Completed:* 1938 (433×40¾×15 (max))
4,200/4,900 tD. *Complement:* 309 officers and men. *Armament:* Six
5.9-inch, 10 smaller AA guns. *Armour:* 1-inch belts; 1½-inch deck.
Propulsion: Twin screw. Parsons single-reduction-geared turbines: 56,000 shp:
32 knots. During WWII TROMP was serving in the East Indies with ships of
the British and American Fleets and was in action in 1942 off Sumatra, being
badly damaged by Japanese destroyers. She was repaired in Australia and in
1944 became one of Admiral Somerville's newly formed Eastern Fleet. In
1957 TROMP became an accommodation ship at Den Helder and in 1969 she
was broken up.

146
GÖTA LEJON Sweden 'Tre Kroner' Class Cruiser. *Completed:* 1947
(597×54×19½) *Complement:* 455 officers and men. *Armament:* Seven
6-inch (one triple and two twin turrets) and 27 40mm Bofors AA guns. Six
21-inch torpedo tubes. *A/S Weapons:* Two depth charge throwers. *Armour:*
5-inch belt. *Propulsion:* Twin screws driven by De Laval double-reduction-
geared turbines: 100,000 shp: 33 knots. Four 4-drum boilers. GÖTA LEJON
was specially designed for service in the Baltic Sea and was equipped to lay
160 mines. In 1971 she was sold to Chile becoming their ALMIRANTE
LATORRE.

147

148

149

147
MONTCALM France C 'Gloire' Class. *Completed:* 1937
(580¾×57½×17½) 7,600/10,850 tD. *Complement:* 674 officers and men.
Armament: nine 6-inch, eight 3.5-inch AA, 40 smaller AA guns. Four
21¼-inch torpedo tubes. *Armour:* 4-inch belt, 5½-inch turrets, and lighter
protection elsewhere. *Propulsion:* Twin screws: Parsons single-reduction-
geared turbines: 84,000shp: 31 knots. Originally six ships in the class but
three were scuttled at Toulon during the fall of France in WWII. In 1959
MONTCALM became a stationary training ship at Toulon and was
withdrawn 10 years later.

148
MIGUEL DE CERVANTES Spain C. *Completed:* 1931
(579½×54×16½) 8,250/9,900 tD. *Complement:* 564 officers and men.
Armament: Eight 6-inch in twin turrets, eight 5.5-inch AA and 20 smaller AA
guns. *Armour:* 3-inch belt, 2-inch side forward and lighter armour elsewhere.
1-inch deck. *Propulsion:* Parsons single-reduction-geared turbines: 80,000
shp: 33 knots. There were two similar ships and all three were extensively
refitted and modernised after the Civil War in 1940-46. They were also, later,
re-armed.

149
ALMIRANTE BARROSO Brazil C Ex USS PHILADELPHIA
'Brooklyn' Class. *Completed:* 1938. Sold to Brazil 1951. (608½×69×19¾)
9,700/13,000 tD. *Complement:* About 900 officers and men. *Armament:* 15
6-inch guns in triple turrets; eight 5-inch in twin turrets and 52 20mm and
40mm AA guns. *Armour:* 4-inch belt, 3-inch deck, 5-inch turrets and 8-inch
conning tower. *Propulsion:* Quadruple screw — Westinghouse single-
reduction-geared turbines: 100,000 shp: 32½ knots. There was a hangar for
four aircraft with spares right aft on the main deck. A large crane lifted the
aircraft off the hatch in the quarter deck and placed them on one of two
catapults. These were removed before the ship was at Spithead.

150

BALTIMORE USA Heavy Cruiser. *Completed:* 1943 (673½×71×26 (max)) 13,600/17,200 tD. *Complement:* 1,700 officers and men.
Armament: Nine 8-inch in triple turrets. 12 5-inch AA and 75 smaller guns. One helicopter. *Armour:* 6-inch belt; 3-inch decks. *Propulsion:* Quadruple screws: General Electric single-reduction-geared turbines: 120,000 shp: 34 knots. Four Babcock boilers. There were 14 ships in the class. They each had a hangar right aft below the quarter deck with a hatch above it and one or two large cranes at the stern. Originally two catapults were fitted but these were removed and the four aircraft replaced by a helicopter. BALTIMORE was scrapped in 1972.

151

152

151
SVERDLOV USSR C One of a Class of about 14 ships. *Completed:*
(about) 1952 (689×70×16). *Complement:* 1,050 officers and men.
Armament: 12 5.9-inch guns in four triple turrets. 12 3.9-inch in six twin
mountings: 32 37mm AA. 10 21-inch torpedo tubes in quintuple mountings.
SVERDLOV is fitted for minelaying and can carry about 200 mines.
Armour: Very heavily protected with 4-6-inch belt, 5-inch on turrets, 6-inch
conning tower and lighter armour elsewhere. *Propulsion:* Twin screws driven
by geared turbines: 130,000 shp: 34½ knots.

152
SVERDLOV   The control tower and anti-aircraft bridge.

153
AMERIGO VESPUCCI Italy Sail Training Ship. *Completed:* 1930 (330×51×22) 3,543 tD. *Complement:* 400 officers and men plus 150 midshipmen under training. *Armament:* Four 3-inch and one 20mm AA guns. *Propulsion:* Single screw with diesel-electric drive: 1,900shp: 10½ knots. Sails: 22,600sq ft of canvas. She has a steel hull, masts and spars.

154

155

156

154
CONSUL (ex DUKE OF DEVONSHIRE) 277 tG. 1896. Two cylinder diagonal compound engine: 12 knots. Leaving Southampton with sightseers for the Spithead Review.

155
EMPEROR OF INDIA (ex PRINCESS ROYAL) PS 534 tG. 1906. Two cylinder diagonal compound engine: 14 knots. Leaving Southampton for Spithead.

156
MEDWAY QUEEN PS 316 tG. 1924 Two cylinder diagonal compound engine: 15 knots. She took sightseers round the assembled ships and finished the day as a grandstand. Her normal itinerary was Rochester-Herne Bay-Southend-Rochester.

157

158

157
ST PATRICK SS 3,482 tG. 1948. Twin screw: single-reduction-geared
turbines: 20 knots. Carried a full complement of passengers around the
assembled ships and then anchored to give them all a grandstand view of the
Review.

158
BRITTANY SS 1,522 tG 1933. Twin screw: single-reduction-geared
turbines: 16 knots. Built for the Jersey-France services of the Southern
Railway, she was present at the Reviews of 1935, 1937 and 1953. She is seen
here leaving Southampton with a full load of spectators for the 1953 Review.
After passing through the lines she anchored at the head of 'J' line.

NATO Naval Review 1969

The Naval Review which took place at Spithead on Friday, 16 May, 1969, was held to celebrate 20 years of the North Atlantic Treaty Organisation (NATO) which came into being on 4 April 1949. Signatories to the Treaty were Belgium, Canada, Denmark, France, Iceland, Italy, Luxembourg, Netherlands, Norway, Portugal, United Kingdom and United States of America. Greece and Turkey joined the Alliance in 1952 and West Germany in 1955. The headquarters of the Organisation were in Paris but, after the withdrawal of France in 1966 they were moved to Brussels.

At Spithead, ships of all the NATO Maritime Powers except those of Iceland, were assembled for Review by HM Queen Elizabeth II, at the invitation of those Powers. Six ships of five nations formed the NATO Standing Force Atlantic, a permanent international squadron working and training together for immediate action in an emergency. The total number of ships at the Review was 61, of which the United Kingdom was represented by 14. The largest ship present was the Aircraft Carrier USS WASP: the largest British ship was the Cruiser HMS BLAKE. The majority were smaller ships, there being 17 destroyers, 18 frigates and 15 minesweepers, comprising 50 out of the 61 ships present.

No merchant ships were at the Review except those few local ferries and pleasure ships which carried sightseers to the ceremony and afterwards cruised round the fleets. No official programme of the event was issued but the *Portsmouth News* produced a very informative Souvenir Edition.

The was the first occasion on which the Queen had carried out a review at Spithead from the Royal Yacht BRITANNIA which was escorted by HMS WAKEFUL and the Belgian Navy Support Ship ZINNIA. After the Review many of the ships moved into Portsmouth Harbour and a number were open to the public on the following days.

1969

Ship	Type	Ship	Type
ALCIDE	S/M	KOELSCH	E/D
ALLEN M SUMNER	D	LAFFEY	D
ALMIRANTE PEREIRA		LETTERSTON	M/S
DA SILVA	F	MALMEDY	M/S
ANDREA DORIA	C	McCLOY	E/D
ASPIS	D	MOËN	M/S
AUGSBERG	F	NOORD BRABAND	D
BARNEY	D	OLMEDA	O/T
BAYERN	D	OLYMPUS	S/M
BERGEN	F	OSLO	F
BLAKE	C	PHOEBE	F
BRAUNSCHWEIG	F	PROVIDER	O/T
BREYDEL	F	PUMA	F
CHARLEROI	M/S	ROCHEFORT	M/S
CHUKAWAN	O/T	ROTTERDAM	D
CLAUDE V RICKETTS	D	SEA POACHER	S/M
COMMANDANTE	F	SHOULTON	M/H
HERMENE/GILDO CAPELO		ST LAURENT	E/D
DE ALPINO	F	TENBY	F
DE RUYTER	C	TIPTOE	S/M
DEWEY	F	TONGEREN	M/S
DIDO	F	TORQUAY	F
DINANT	M/S	TRUFFAUT	M/S(O)
EASTBOURNE	F	TURNHOUT	M/S
EVERTSEN	F	VAN NES	F
FRASER	D	VESOLE	D
GATINEAU	E/D	VISE	M/S
GAZIANTEP	D	VOGE	E/D
GLAMORGAN	D	WAKEFUL	F
HEIST	M/S	WASP	A/C
HOLLAND	D	ZEELAND	D
KNOKKE	M/S	ZINNIA	SUP.

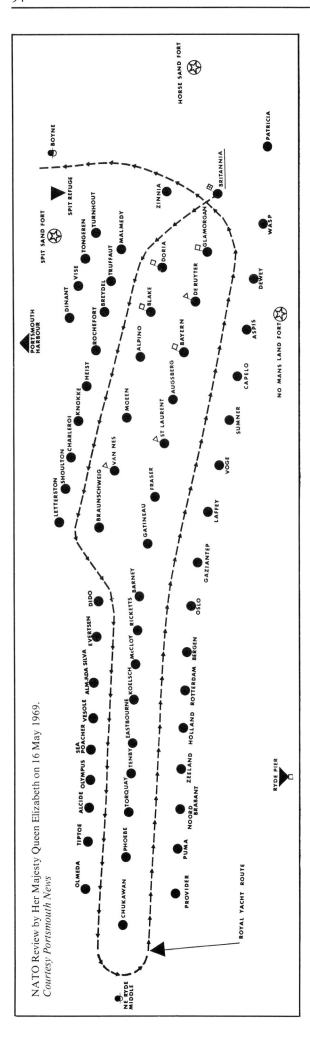

NATO Review by Her Majesty Queen Elizabeth on 16 May 1969.
Courtesy Portsmouth News

159

BRITANNIA Royal Yacht Can be converted to a Hospital Ship in time of war. *Completed:* 1954 (412¼×55×15½) 3,990/4,961 tD. (5,769 tG). *Complement:* 271 officers and men including a Royal Marine Band. She is commanded by a Rear Admiral. *Propulsion:* Twin screws. Single-reduction-geared turbines; 12,000 shp: 21 knots. BRITANNIA has Denny-Brown stabilisers. Her bridge and funnel are of aluminium. She has three masts to

enable her to fly the correct flags on ceremonial occasions. The flag of the Lord High Admiral is at the foremast head, the Royal Standard is flown at the mainmast and the Union Flag at the mizzen. The main topmast and the aerials on the foremast can be struck enabling her to negotiate the bridges of the St Lawrence Seaway. When not required for her royal duties, BRITANNIA takes part in exercises with the Fleet.

160

161

162

160

EASTBOURNE A/S Frigate Type 12 'Whitby' Class. *Completed:* 1957
(369¾×41×17 (max)) 2,150/2,560 tD. *Complement:* 221 officers and men:
as training ship 50 cadets are carried for sea training. *Armament:* Two
4.5-inch HA/LA guns in twin mountings: two 40mm Bofors AA guns.
A/S Weapons: Two Limbo depth charge mortars, each 3-barrelled.
Propulsion: Twin screws: double-reduction-geared steam turbines: 30,430 shp:
31 knots. Two Babcock and Wilcox boilers providing superheated steam at
550 psi and 850°F. Very efficient ships with splendid sea-keeping qualities.
EASTBOURNE with TENBY, TORQUAY and SCARBOROUGH formed
the Dartmouth Training Squadron, EASTBOURNE being the Leader. (See
also Plate 221).

161

TENBY A/S Frigate Type 12 'Whitby' Class. *Completed:* 1957
Description and details as for EASTBOURNE (Plate 160). One of the
Dartmouth Training Squadron ships. Broken up 1977.

162

TORQUAY A/S Frigate Type 12 'Whitby' Class. *Completed:* 1956
Description and details as for EASTBOURNE (Plate 160). One of the
Dartmouth Training Squadron ships.

163

164

165

166

167

163

PUMA AA Frigate Type 41 'Leopard' Class. *Completed:* 1957
($339\frac{3}{4} \times 40 \times 16$ (max)) 2,300/2,520 tD. *Complement:* 205 officers and men.
Armament: Four 4.5-inch HA/LA guns in twin turrets: one 40mm AA.
A/S Weapons: One Squid 3-barrelled depth charge mortar. *Propulsion:* Twin
screws: four Admiralty Type 1 diesel engines, two geared to each shaft: 12,380
bhp: 25 knots. Stabilised. All welded hull. The ship was refitted in 1964 and
given a 'combined mast and stack'. All four ships of the class were so altered.
PUMA was of great help to the people of Tristan da Cunha when they
returned to their island after the volcanic eruption there. After the Review she
was at Chatham for disposal. Broken up 1976.

164

DIDO Frigate — 'Leander' Class. *Completed:* 1963 ($372 \times 41 \times 18$ (max))
2,450/2,860 tD *Complement:* 263 officers and men. *Armament:* Two
4.5-inch HA/LA guns in twin turret. Two 40mm and two 20mm Bofors AA
guns. *A/S Weapons:* One 3-barrelled Limbo depth charge mortar. One
helicopter with homing torpedoes. Equipped with VDS. *Propulsion:* Twin
screws driven by double-reduction-geared steam turbines: 30,000 shp: 30
knots. DIDO was allocated to the NATO Standing Naval Force, Atlantic.

165

PHOEBE Frigate 'Leander' Class. *Completed:* 1966. Description and
details as for the earlier ship DIDO (Plate 164) except that the 40mm Bofors
guns are replaced by one Seacat (short range AA) quadruple missile launcher.
(See also Plate 214).

166

GLAMORGAN Guided Missile Destroyer 'County' Class. *Completed:*
1966 ($520\frac{1}{2} \times 54 \times 20$ (max)) 5,440/6,200 tD. *Complement:* 471 officers and
men. *Armament:* Four 4.5-inch HA/LA guns in twin turrets forward of the
bridge: two 20mm AA guns. One Seaslug surface to air twin launcher: two
Seacat (short range surface to air) quadruple missile launchers. One helicopter
with hangar and launching platform abaft the after funnel. *Propulsion:*
COSAG twin screws, each shaft driven by single-reduction-geared steam
turbines HP and LP) developing 15,000 shp and two gas turbines developing
the same horsepower. Total 60,000 shp: $32\frac{1}{2}$ knots. The two types of power
can each be used separately or together. Two boilers providing superheated
steam at 700 psi and 950°F. These eight handsome ships although called
'Destroyers' are more than the equal of many cruisers of former times.

167

BLAKE (ex TIGER ex BLAKE) Command Helicopter Cruiser
($566\frac{1}{2} \times 64 \times 23$) 9,500/12,080 tD. *Complement:* 885 officers and men.
Completed: (As a cruiser of improved SUPERB Class) 1961. Laid down 1942,
launched 1945. Work stopped on BLAKE and two sister ships, from 1946
until 1954, when design was altered. *Armament:* As completed she had four
6-inch HA/LA guns in two turrets in 'A' and 'X' positions. Rebuilt as
Helicopter Cruiser 1965-1969 with a hangar aft for four Sea King helicopters
and a large launching pad. This involved the removal of the 6-inch turret from
'X' position and now, she has only the forward twin turret and two 3-inch AA
guns in a twin turret in 'B' position. She has two quadruple Seacat missile
systems. *Armour:* $3\frac{1}{2}$-inch belt: 4-inch conning tower. 2-inch turrets and
deck. *Propulsion:* Quadruple screws: Parsons single-reduction-geared steam
turbines: 80,000 shp: $31\frac{1}{2}$ knots. Four Admiralty 3-drum boilers with
superheaters. W.P. 400 psi. The machinery can be remotely controlled. The
electricity supply is alternating current. The ship is fully air conditioned. In
1980 she was laid up at Chatham. (See also Plates 201 and 202).

168

169

168
FRASER Canada D. *Completed:* 1957 (366×42×13½) 2,263/2,800 tD. *Complement:* 250 officers and men. *Armament:* Two 3-inch HA/LA in twin mounts. *A/S Weapons:* One 3-barrelled Limbo depth charge mortar. One A/S helicopter. *Propulsion:* Single-reduction-geared steam turbines driving twin screws: 30,000 shp: 28½ knots. The fitting of a helicopter hangar and launching platform abaft the funnel in 1965-6 involved the removal of a 3-inch gun and one Limbo. FRASER and her six sister ships of the 'St Laurent' Class have Variable Depth Sonar (VDS). Much of their superstructure is of aluminium but the forward gun-shield is made of fibre glass.

169
PROVIDER Canada Helicopter Carrier and Supply Ship. *Completed:* 1963 (555×76×32 (max)) 7,300/22,700 tD. 20,000 tG. *Complement:* 142 officers and men. *Propulsion:* Single screw driven by double-reduction-geared steam turbines: 21,000 shp: 20 knots. There is a large helicopter platform aft with hangars for three helicopters situated below the funnel. For the movement of supplies, 20 electro-hydraulic winches and a self-propelled vehicle are provided. There is a well-equipped 8-berth hospital in the forward bridge structure which also contains the captain's accommodation and the usual navigational spaces — chart room and control room.

170

171

170/171
BRAUNSCHWEIG   West Germany   Fast Frigate   'Koln' Class.
Completed: 1964   (361×36¼×11¼)   2,100/2,550 tD   *Complement:* 210
officers and men.   *Armament:* Two 3.9-inch HA/LA and six 40mm AA
guns.   *A/S Weapons:* Two 4-barrelled depth charge mortars. Two torpedo
tubes for ASW torpedoes.   *Propulsion:* Twin screw cpp CODAG: Four
12,000 bhp MAN diesels and one 24,000 bhp gas turbine geared to each shaft.
Total 36,000 bhp: 32 knots.   There are six ships in this class, all named after
German towns. (See AUGSBURG, Plate 172.) BRAUNSCHWEIG was one
of the NATO Standing Force, Atlantic.

172

173

172
AUGSBERG West Germany Fast Frigate. 'Koln' Class. *Completed:*
1962 For description and details see BRAUNSCHWEIG (Plates 170/171).
AUGSBURG, however, was not attached to the NATO Standing Naval
Force, Atlantic.

173
BAYERN West Germany D 'Hamburg' Class. *Completed:* 1965
($439\frac{3}{4}\times44\times17$) 3,340/4,330 tD. *Complement:* 287 officers and men.
Armament: Four 3.9-inch HA/LA guns in single mountings. Eight 40mm
Bofors AA in twin mountings. Five 21-inch torpedo tubes. *A/S Weapons:*
Two Bofors 4-barrelled rocket launchers. Two torpedo tubes for A/S
torpedoes. *Propulsion:* Double-reduction-geared steam turbines driving twin
screws: 68,000 shp: $35\frac{3}{4}$ knots. Four boilers providing superheated steam at
910 psi and 860°F. A very powerful, fast ship, one of four, all of which were
named after states of the German Federal Republic.

174

175

174
ALPINO (ex CIRCE) Italy F. *Completed* 1968 (381¼×43×12¾) 2,700 full load displacement. *Complement:* 254 officers and men. *Armament:* Six 3-inch HA/LA. *A/S Weapons:* One single barrel depth charge mortar; two triple 12-inch tubes for A/S torpedoes. Two A/S helicopters. The hangar and platform for these are abaft the funnel. *Propulsion:* twin screws. CODAG — four diesels, two to each shaft — 16,800 hp and two gas turbines one geared to each shaft — 15,000. Total 31,800 hp: 28 knots.

175
ANDREA DORIA. Italy. Guided Missile Escort Cruiser. *Completed:* 1964 (489¾×56½×16½) 6,500 tons full load displacement. *Complement:* 478 officers and men. *Armament:* Eight 3-inch AA guns. One Terrier ship-to-air twin missile launcher. Six 12-inch torpedo tubes in triple mounts for A/S torpedoes. Four A/S helicopters with launching pad aft. *Propulsion:* Twin screws: double-reduction-geared steam turbines: 60,000 shp: 30 knots. Four Foster-Wheeler boilers providing superheated steam at 711 psi and 842°F. The ship is stabilised.

176

177

178

176
HOLLAND Netherlands A/S Destroyer 'Holland' Class. *Completed:*
1955 (371×37½×16¾) 2,215/2,765 tD. *Complement:* 247 officers and
men. *Armament:* Four 4.7-inch guns in twin turrets: one 40mm AA gun.
A/S Weapons: Four 4-barrelled depth charge mortars. *Propulsion:* Twin
screws driven by Parsons single-reduction-geared steam turbines; 45,000 shp:
32 knots. The engines of the four 'Holland' Class were manufactured in
Holland for four destroyers which were to have been built by the Germans in
Netherlands shipyards. These were never built and the complete power
installations for them were found intact after the war. She was sold to Peru in
1978.

177
NOORD BRABAND Netherlands. A/S Destroyer. 'Holland' Class.
Completed: 1955: Description and details as for HOLLAND (Plate 176).

178
ZEELAND Netherlands A/S Destroyer 'Holland' Class. *Completed:*
1955. Description and details as for HOLLAND (Plate 176)

179

180

181

179

VAN NES Netherlands Frigate. *Completed:* 1967 (372×41×18) 2,200/
2,850 tD *Complement:* 254 officers and men. *Armament:* Two 4.5-inch HA/
LA in twin turret. Two Seacat quadruple launchers. *A/S Weapons:* One
3-barrelled depth charge mortar. One helicopter with homing torpedoes.
Propulsion: Twin screws powered by double-reduction-geared steam turbines:
30,000 shp: 28½ knots. This ship and her sister ship EVERTSEN are nearly
identical with the British frigates of the 'Leander' Class (qv).

180

EVERTSEN Netherlands Frigate *Completed:* 1967. For description and
details see VAN NES (Plate 180). Both ships were attached to the NATO
Standing Force, Atlantic.

181

ROTTERDAM A/S Destroyer 'Friesland' class. *Completed:* 1957
(380½×38½×17) 2,497/3,070 tD *Complement:* 284 officers and men.
Armament: Four 4.7-inch HA/LA. Two 40mm AA guns. *A/S Weapons:*
Four Limbo 4-barrelled depth charge mortars. *Armour:* These ships have
some light side and deck protection. *Propulsion:* Twin screw: single-
reduction-geared steam turbines: 60,000 shp: 36 knots. There were eight
ships in the class.

182

183

182

DE RUYTER Netherlands C. *Completed:* 1953. She was laid down in 1939, launched by the occupying Germans in 1944 as DE ZEVEN PROVINCIEN ($614\frac{1}{2} \times 56\frac{1}{4} \times 22$ (max)) 9,529/11,850 tD. *Complement:* 926 officers and men. *Armament:* Eight 6-inch guns in twin turrets; eight 57mm also in twin turrets and eight smaller AA guns. *Propulsion:* Twin screws driven by Parsons single-reduction-geared steam turbines: 85,000 shp: 32 knots. DE RUYTER was sold to Peru in 1975 and replaced by two destroyers.

183

BERGEN Norway Frigate (Destroyer Escort). *Completed:* 1967 ($317 \times 36\frac{1}{4} \times 17\frac{1}{2}$) 1,450/1,745 tD. *Complement:* 151 officers and men. *Armament:* Four 3-inch HA/LA in twin mounts. *A/S Weapons:* Two Terne system torpedo launchers. *Propulsion:* single screw; De Laval double-reduction-geared steam turbines; 20,000 shp: 25 knots. There are five ships in this, the 'Oslo' Class. They are of US design and half the cost of their construction was borne by the USA.

184

185

184
GAZIANTEP Turkey D 'Gelibolu' Class. *Completed:* 1942 as USS
LANSDOWNE. Transferred to Turkey in 1950 $(348\frac{1}{2} \times 36 \times 18$ (max))
1,810/2,580 tD. *Complement:* 250 officers and men. *Armament:* Four
5-inch in single mountings and four 40mm AA guns. Five 21-inch torpedo
tubes. *A/S Weapons:* Two Hedgehog ATW: Four depth charge throwers:
homing torpedoes. *Propulsion:* General Electric (USA) single-reduction-
geared steam turbines: twin screws: 50,000 shp: 34 knots. GAZIANTEP
was modernised in the USA in 1958 and, in 1980, was returned to the US
Navy for duties as a target ship.

185
406 SEA POACHER USA 'Balao' Class submarine One of a series of 115
boats built in 1944. It made several patrols into enemy water before the end of
WWII. 10 sister boats were sunk by enemy action. SEA POACHER is one of
30 of the class which, during 1952-54, were reconstructed and modernised
under the Greater Underwater Propulsion Project and which became known
as the GUPPY boats. None now remain in the US Navy but a number are still
active in the navies of other nations: SEA POACHER was sold in July 1974
to Peru. Standard displacement: 1,840 tons; Submerged 2,445 tons. Twin
screws: Surface power: three diesels — 18 knots. Submerged two electric
motors — 15 knots. 10 torpedo tubes. Can be used for minelaying.

186

187

188

186

LAFFEY USA D. *Completed:* 1944, but extensively modernised under the Fleet Rehabilitation and Modernisation programme (FRAM II) (376½×41×19) 2,200/3,320 tD. *Complement:* 274 officers and men. *Armament:* Six 5-inch HA/LA guns. *A/S Weapons:* Two triple A/S torpedo launchers: two fixed torpedo tubes: two Hedgehogs: two drone A/S helicopters (DASH). *Propulsion:* Twin screws: single-reduction-geared steam turbines: 60,000 shp: 34 knots. During WWII LAFFEY was hit eight times by Japanese 'suicide planes' and survived. In 1945 the ship was awarded a Presidential citation.

187

VESOLE USA Fleet Escort Destroyer, modernised 'Gearing' Class, FRAM I. *Completed:* 1945 (390½×41×19) 2,425/3,480 tD. *Complement:* 274 officers and men. *Armament:* Four 5-inch HA/LA guns.

A/S Weapons: One ASROC eight-tube launcher. Two triple torpedo launchers. *Propulsion:* Twin screws: single-reduction-geared steam turbines: 60,000 shp: 34 knots. VESOLE was a conversion from a Radar Picket Destroyer. She was attached to NATO Standing Naval Force, Atlantic.

188

BARNEY USA Guided Missile Destroyer. 'Charles F. Adams' Class. *Completed:* 1962 (437×47×20) 3,370/4,500 tD. *Complement:* 354 officers and men. *Armament:* One twin Tartar (SAM) missile launcher. Two 5-inch HA/LA guns. *A/S Weapons:* One ASROC 8-tube launcher; two triple torpedo launchers. *Propulsion:* Twin screw: Westinghouse single-reduction-geared turbines: 70,000 shp: 35 knots. The superstructure is of aluminium. The ship is completely air conditioned.

189
CLAUDE V. RICKETTS (ex BIDDLE '64) USA Guided Missile
Destroyer. *Completed:* 1962. Description and details as for BARNEY
(Plate 187).

190

DEWEY USA Guided Missile Frigate 'Coontz' Class. *Completed:* 1959 (512½×52½×25) 4,700/5,800 tD. *Complement:* 375 officers and men. *Armament:* One 5-inch HA/LA, four 3-inch AA guns. One twin Terrier missile launcher. *A/S Weapons:* One ASROC 8-tube launcher: two triple A/S torpedo launchers. *Propulsion:* Twin screw: Allis-Chalmers single-reduction-geared steam turbines: 85,000 shp: 34 knots All ships of this class have aluminium superstructures. Soon after leaving the Review, DEWEY entered the Philadelphia Naval Shipyard to undergo modernisation and extension of missile capacity.

191

McCLOY USA Escort Ship. *Completed:* 1963 (371½×40¼×23) 2,360/2,650 tD. *Complement:* 220 officers and men. *Armament:* Three 3-inch AA guns. *A/S Weapons:* One Anti-Submarine Rocket (ASROC) 8-tube launcher: two triple torpedo launchers: two Drone Anti-Submarine helicopters (DASH). *Propulsion:* De Laval single-reduction-geared steam turbines: 20,000 shp: 26 knots. Two ships only in the class. They have a helicopter pad just forward of the after gun.

192

193

192

VOGE USA Escort Ship. *Completed:* 1966 (414½×44¼×24) 2,620/
3,400 tD. *Complement:* 241 officers and men. *Armament:* Two 5-inch HA/
LA guns. *A/S Weapons:* One ASROC (anti-submarine rocket) launcher (8
tubes): two triple torpedo launchers and two fixed torpedo tubes in the stern.
The A/S missiles are computer controlled. *Propulsion:* Single screw:
Westinghouse single-reduction-geared steam turbines: 35,000 shp: 27 knots.
Two Foster-Wheeler boilers of advanced design providing superheated steam
at 1,200 psi. VOGE and her sister ship KOELSH were the most modern
United States ships at the Review.

193

KOELSCH USA Escort Ship. *Completed:* 1967. For description and
details see VOGE (Plate 191).

194

195

194
WASP (ex ORISKANY) USA ASW Support A/C 'Essex' Class.
Completed: 1943 (890×102×31) Width of flight deck 196ft (max) 33,000/
40,600 (approx) tD. *Complement:* (approx) 2,400-1,615 officers and men
plus about 800 ASW personnel. *Armament:* Four 5-inch HA/LA. *Aircraft:*
40-47 including up to 20 helicopters. Angled flight deck with two hydraulic
catapults. *Propulsion:* Quadruple screws driven by Westinghouse single-
reduction-geared steam turbines. Eight boilers working at 600 psi. WASP
was converted from an attack aircraft carrier to ASW Support in 1955 during
the second Fleet Rehabilitation and Modernisation Programme (Fram II).
WASP was the largest ship at the NATO Review and wore the flag of Rear
Admiral F.B. Stone in command of all the American ships present. During
WWII she served in the Pacific and was badly damaged by a bomb from a
Japanese aircraft. In 1965 she was the 'rescue ship' for the Gemini Space
Mission. WASP was broken up in 1973.

195
CHUKAWAN USA Oiler. *Completed:* 1946 (553×75×31½) 25,525 full
load displacement. *Complement:* 64 officers and men. *Armament:* One
5-inch and four 3-inch guns. *Propulsion:* Twin screws: single-reduction-
geared turbines: 13,500 shp: 18 knots. CHUKAWAN was one of a class of
25 oilers built between 1939 and 1946. Two of the ships were sunk during
WWII. Three others have been lengthened 91 feet by the insertion of an extra
tank section amidships. CHUKAWAN supplied the US Sixth Fleet during the
Lebanon crisis in 1958. In 1969 she was attached to the Atlantic Fleet and
carried a blue letter 'E' as an award for 'efficiency'.

Silver Jubilee Review 1977

The Silver Jubilee of Her Majesty Queen Elizabeth II was celebrated by the Royal Navy in a Review of the Fleet at Spithead on Tuesday, 28 June 1977. Ninety-eight ships were present and there were 53 ships of the Merchant Navy and the Royal Fleet Auxiliary. In addition, 20 warships from Allied and Commonwealth navies were present.

The largest naval ships were the Aircraft Carrier ARK ROYAL, the ASW and Assault Carrier, HERMES, and the Aircraft Carrier MELBOURNE of the Royal Australian Navy. In general, however, except for the carriers, two cruisers and an assault ship, it was a Review of smaller ships, the majority being frigates and destroyers although some of the latter are larger than many cruisers of earlier days.

The first ships, those of the Royal Navy, began to assemble on Friday, 24 June to be followed the next day by ships of the Commonwealth and Allied navies. The fleets were illuminated for two hours from 2200 hours on each of the three nights, 25 to 27 June and for four hours on the day of the Review when there was also a firework display.

On 28 June, the Review commenced at 1425 hours. The Queen and members of the Royal Family sailing in the Royal Yacht BRITANNIA preceded by the Trinity House Yacht PATRICIA and followed by HMS BIRMINGHAM carrying members of the Board of Admiralty. Next in the procession came the Royal Fleet Auxiliaries LYNESS, SIR GERAINT and SIR TRISTRAM carrying official guests, Members of Parliament and other invited persons. Last in the procession came the Helicopter Support Ship ENGADINE carrying the Press. For most of the five days, the weather was cold, windy and often wet and this obviously presented problems for the fly-past of fixed wing aircraft. Helicopters, however, were able to maintain excellent formation during their fly-past in two waves.

The Silver Jubilee Review was noteworthy in that it was the first such occasion (excluding the NATO Review) at which there was no battleship and at which nuclear-powered ships were present. When it was considered that nearly all of British naval power was on review, that 30 of the ships were small minesweepers and that a number of the remainder were either in reserve or engaged in non-combatant duties such as training, the ranks began to look very thin indeed. Furthermore, the armament of most ships is mainly of a *de*fensive nature (*anti*-submarine, *anti*-aircraft, *anti*-surface ship), and one could only hope and believe that some of those weapons could be used offensively when the occasion demanded.

For the first time it was seen that all the modern combatant ships were equipped with various types of missile launchers though it was said that no ship had its full complement of missiles, a fact which seemed to be borne out by even casual inspection. However, a number of ships had the 'Corvus' counter-measure system from which 'chaff' can be fired to cause deviation in the aim of attacking missiles.

Of the visiting warships, the most interesting was the United States nuclear-powered Cruiser CALIFORNIA which was also the largest Allied ship present. Of the smaller Allied ships the Netherlands Destroyer TROMP was impressive as being exceedingly well armed and equipped for a ship of her size (4,300/5,400 tD).

Many yachts and pleasure boats sailed continuously round the anchored ships while tugs, fleet tenders and other small craft were busy at all times acting as ferries between the Dockyard and the ships. Altogether a very impressive and interesting occasion.

1977

Ship	Type	Ship	Type	Ship	Type	Ship	Type
ALACRITY	F	GLAMORGAN	D	PHOEBE	F	STROMNESS	RFA
ALFRISTON	FP	GLASSERTON	MCM	PLYMOUTH	F	(Stores Support Ship)	
AMAZON	F	GOLD ROVER	RFA	PORTISHAM	D/T	SUPERB	F S/M
ANDROMEDA	F	(Fleet Tanker)		PUTTENHAM	D/T	TARTAR	F
ANTELOPE	F	GOOSANDER	BV	RECLAIM	D/S	THAKENHAM	D/T
ANTRIM	D	GURKHA	F	ROTHESAY	F	TIDESPRING	RFA
APOLLO	F	HARDY	F	ROYSTERER	TUG	(Fleet Tanker)	
ARETHUSA	F	HECATE	CS	SABRE	FTB	TIGER	H/C
ARIADNE	F	HECLA	CS	SCYLLA	F	TONGHAM	F/T RNAS
ARK ROYAL	A/C	HERALD	S/S	SALISBURY	F	TORQUAY	F
ARROW	F	HERMES	VSTOL/C	SCIMITAR	FTB	UPTON	RNR
AUDEMER	LCT	HERMIONE	F	SEALION	P S/M	VALIANT	F S/M
BEAGLE	CS	HODGESTON	RNR	SHAVINGTON	M/S	WALRUS	F S/M
BERWICK	F	ISIS	M/H	SHEFFIELD	D	WATERWITCH	M/S
BILDESTON	MCM	IVESTON	M/S	SHIPHAM	F/T	WILTON	MCM
BIRMINGHAM	D	JUPITER	F	SHOULTON	MCM	WISTON	RNR
BLAKE	H/C	KEDLESTON	RNR	SIR GERAINT	RFA	WOODLARK	M/S
BOSSINGTON	MCM	KELLINGTON	RNR	(Logistic Landing Ship)		ZULU	F
BRIGHTON	F	KENT	D	SIR TRISTRAM	RFA		
BRINTON	M/H (FP)	LALESTON	M/S	(Logistic Landing Ship)			
BULLDOG	CS	LONDON	D				
CACHALOT	P S/M	LOYAL CHANCELLOR					
CHARYBDIS	F		F/T				
CHURCHILL	F S/M	LOYAL MODERATOR	F/T	**Foreign Warships**			
CLEOPATRA	F	LOYAL PROTECTOR	F/T	Name	Type		Country
CROFTON	RNR	LYNESS	RFA				
CUTLAS	FTB	(Stores Support Ship)		ALMIRANTE			
CUXTON	M/S (FP)	LYNX	F	MAGALHAES			
DANAE	F	MAXTON	MCM	CORREA	F		Portugal
DEVONSHIRE	D	NAIAD	F	ARDITO	D		Italy
DIOMEDE	F	NEWTON	T/S RMA	BERK	D		Turkey
DITTISHAM	M/S	NUBIAN	F	BILLFISH	S/M SSN		USA
DREADNOUGHT	F S/M	NURTON	MCM	BRISBANE	D		Australia
DUNDAS	F	OCELOT	P S/M	CALIFORNIA	C		USA
EASTBOURNE	F	OLWEN	RFA	CANTERBURY	F		New Zealand
ECHO	IS/V	(Fleet Tanker)		DUQUESNE	C		France
EGERIA	IS/V	OPOSSUM	P S/M	GODETIA	Support Ship		Belgium
ENGADINE	RFA	OPPORTUNE	P S/M	HAMBURG	D		Federal German
(Helicopter Support Ship)		ORACLE	P S/M				Republic
ENTERPRISE	IS/V	ORPHEUS	P S/M	HURON	D		Canada
EURYALUS	F	OSIRIS	P S/M	KAMAN	Fast Attack craft		Iran
FAWN	CS	OTUS	P S/M	LT TROUPAKIS	Fast Attack craft		Greece
FEARLESS	Assault Ship	PAGHAM	F/T	MELBOURNE	A/C		Australia
FIFE	D	PATRICIA		MØEN	M/LR		Denmark
FLINTHAM	M/S	TRINITY HOUSE		NARVIK	F		Norway
FOX	CS	PEARLEAF	RFA	PAHLAWAN	Fast Attack craft		Brunei
GALATEA	F	(Fleet Tanker)		TROMP	D		Netherlands
GAVINTON	MCM	PETEREL	RNR	UDAYGIRI	F		India
				ZUBIN	Fast Attack craft		Iran

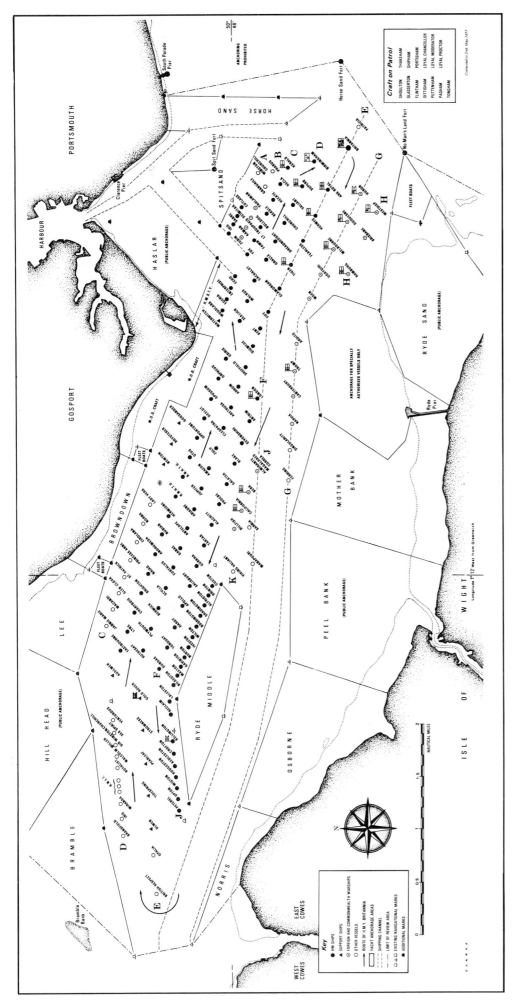

Silver Jubilee Review of the Fleet by Her Majesty Queen Elizabeth on 2 May
1977. *Courtesy Navy International*

196

197

196
ARK ROYAL (ex IRRESISTIBLE) Aircraft Carrier. *Completed:* 1955
(845×166×36 Width of hull: 112¾) 43,060/50,786 tD. *Complement:* 2,640
officers and men including Air staff. *Armour:* 4.5-inch belts: 4-inch flight
deck: 2.5-inch hangar deck and 1.5-inch hangar sides *Catapults:* Two
improved steam. *Aircraft:* 30 fixed wing and 6 helicopters. *Propulsion:* Four
screws: single-reduction-geared steam turbines: 152,000 shp: 31½ knots.
ARK ROYAL was originally almost a sister ship to EAGLE (Plate 95) but in
a very costly refit in 1967-70 she was largely reconstructed with an angled
flight deck. She had no fixed armament though provision was made for four
quadruple Seacat (surface to air) launchers but these were never fitted. This
view shows her ship's Company 'manning the rails' in rehearsal for the actual
Review next day. She was withdrawn from the active list in 1979 and broken
up in 1980.

197
ARK ROYAL Aircraft Carrier. This bow view gives a good idea of her size
and the width of her flight deck. At the Silver Jubilee Review ARK ROYAL
was the Fleet Flagship.

198

199

198

HERMES (ex ELEPHANT) Helicopter and Vertical Short Take-off and Landing (V/STOL) Carrier. *Completed:* 1959 (744¼×160×29 width of hull 90) 23,900/28,800 tD. *Complement:* 980 officers and men. *Armament:* Missiles: Two quadruple Seacat (surface to air) launchers on each side of the ship. *Armour:* The flight deck is reinforced. *Aircraft:* 20 Wessex Sea King and four Sioux helicopters. *Propulsion:* Twin screws driven by single-reduction-geared steam turbines: 76,000 shp: 28 knots. HERMES was laid down as a carrier of the 'Centaur' Class but was modified and modernised during construction with an angled flight deck and other improvements. During 1971-73 she was converted to a Commando Carrier with the removal of her catapults and arrester gear. In 1976, however, she was again altered to include an anti-submarine capability. Fitted with ski-jump ramp in 1980.

199

BLAKE (ex TIGER ex BLAKE) for description and details please see those given for the ship in the 1969 Review (Plate 167).

200

TIGER (ex BELLEROPHON) Command Helicopter Cruiser. *Completed:* 1959. Converted from Improved "Superb" Class Cruiser 1968-1972. Other description and details as for BLAKE (Plates 167 and 199).

201

202

201/202

FEARLESS Assault Ship for Amphibious Warfare Forces. *Completed:* 1965 (520×80×20½) 11,060/12,120 tD. *Complement:* 580 officers and men. *Armament:* Two 40mm Bofors AA guns. *Missiles:* Four Seacat surface to air/surface to surface launchers. *Aircraft:* Five Wessex helicopters can be accommodated on deck aft. *Propulsion:* Twin screws driven by single-reduction-geared steam turbines. Two Babcock boilers. The two propulsion units are *en echelon*, the port unit being situated forward of the starboard. FEARLESS and her sister INTREPID can carry tanks, vehicles and up to 400 troops in addition to 700 military personnel for short periods. She can accommodate four landing craft (personnel) on davits and her stern can be ballasted down so that four 'landing craft mechanical' (LCM) can be floated in to her 'dock'. By pumping out the ballast, the stern is raised and the LCM's rest on the dock plating of the mother ship. When ballasted the displacement tonnage of FEARLESS is 16,950. She is used for a training ship for Dartmouth Officers under training when not required for other duties. Plate 201 (top) is a 'bow three quarter' view of the ship and Plate 202 (bottom) is a stern view showing a landing craft in the dock.

203

204

203
ANTRIM Destroyer 'County' Class. *Completed:* 1970 (520½×54×20) 5,440/6,200 tD. *Complement:* 471 officers and men. *Armament:* Guns: Two 4.5-inch HA/LA: Two 20mm AA. *Missiles:* Four Exocet (surface to surface in 'B' gun position forward: two Seacat (surface to air), one on each side of the hangar: twin Seaslug II (surface to air and surface to surface) aft. *Propulsion:* COSAG: twin screws: two single-reduction-geared steam turbines: 30,000 shp: two booster gas turbines 30,000 shp: total of 60,000 shp: 30 knots.   The 'County' Class destroyers are larger and more powerful than most previous light cruisers. The ships are air-conditioned and stabilised.

204
HMS FIFE with GLAMORGAN (right background). The description and details of these 'County' Class Destroyers is the same as those given for ANTRIM (Plate 203).

205

206

205
FIFE Destroyer 'County' Class, showing helicopter and Seaslug II launcher on the quarterdeck. Description and details as for ANTRIM (Plate 203).

206
GLAMORGAN Destroyer 'County' Class. *Completed:* 1977. Showing Seaslug II launcher. Description and detail as for ANTRIM (Plate 203). See also Plate 166 which shows the ship as she was in 1969.

207

208

207

SHEFFIELD Destroyer Type 42. *Completed:* 1975 (410×46×14) 3,150/
3,500 tD. *Complement:* 299 officers and men. *Armament: Guns:* One
4.5-inch HA/LA automatic: two 20mm Oerlikon AA. *Missiles:* One twin Sea
Dart (surface to air/surface to surface) launcher. *A/S Weapons:* Helicopter
launched A/S torpedoes. One Lynx helicopter. *Propulsion:* COGOG —
combination of gas turbines for full power or less powerful gas turbines for
cruising. Two shafts with controllable pitch propellers. 50,000 shp: 30 knots.
This is the first of 14 powerful ships which are stabilised and air conditioned.
They will ultimately be fitted with six A/S torpedo tubes.

208

BIRMINGHAM Destroyer Type 42. *Completed:* 1976. Description and
details as for SHEFFIELD (Plate 207). The second of the class of 14 ships.

209

210

209

AMAZON Frigate Type 21. *Completed:* 1974 (384×41¾×12¼) 2,000/
2,500 tD. *Complement:* 170 officers and men. *Armament: Guns:* One
4.5-inch HA/LA: two 20mm Oerlikon AA. *Missiles:* One quadruple Seacat
(surface to air) launcher. *A/S Weapons:* Six A/S torpedo tubes. One
helicopter with homing torpedoes. *Propulsion:* COGOG: twin controllable
pitch propellors each driven by a Rolls-Royce Olympus gas turbine with a
total of 56,000 shp: 32.2 knots. For cruising, the ship is driven by two Tyne

gas turbines: 8,500shp. This view shows the fine lines of these ships which
were designed and built commercially.

210

AMAZON Frigate Type 21. Showing the helicopter hangar with
quadruple Seacat launcher on its roof.

211

212

211
ALACRITY Frigate Type 21. *Completed:* 1977. Description and details as for AMAZON (Plate 209) but in ALACRITY there are four Exocet (surface to surface) launchers fitted in front of the bridge structure. A quadruple Seacat (surface to air) launcher is mounted on the hangar.

212
ARROW Frigate Type 21. *Completed:* 1976. Description and details as for AMAZON but has Exocet, and Seacat missile systems as ALACRITY (Plate 211).

213

214

215

213

CLEOPATRA Frigate 'Leander' Class. *Completed:* 1966 (372×41×18) 2,450/2,860 tD. *Complement:* 251 officers and men. *Armament: Guns:* Two 40mm AA. *Missiles:* Four Exocet (surface to surface) launchers forward and in place of twin 4.5-inch gun turret. Two Seacat (surface to air) launchers on hangar. *A/S Weapons:* Triple A/S torpedo tubes. One Wasp helicopter with homing torpedoes. *Propulsion:* Twin screws driven by double-reduction-geared steam turbines: 30,000 shp: 30 knots. The 'Leander' Class ships are a development of the Type 12 'Whitby' Class. They have all-welded hulls and are magnificent sea boats. Originally armed with two 4.5-inch HA/LA guns some now have missile launchers, either Exocet or Ikara forward of the bridge.

214

PHOEBE Frigate 'Leander' Class. *Completed:* 1966. Description and details as for CLEOPATRA (Plate 213). The stern well for variable depth sonar (Plate 215) has been plated over. The ship is seen leaving Portsmouth to take station in the Review Anchorage. (See also Plate 165.)

215

ARETHUSA Frigate 'Leander' Class. *Completed:* 1965. Description and details as for CLEOPATRA (Plate 213) but ARETHUSA has Ikara ship-launched A/S torpedo launcher forward in place of Exocet. She also retains her variable depth sonar seen here in the stern well. In this photograph, numerous booms with flood lights attached can be seen projecting over the port side of the ship to provide ARETHUSA's contribution to the flood-lighting of the Fleet after the Review.

216

217

218

216
DIOMEDE Frigate 'Broad Beamed Leander' Class. *Completed:* 1972
(372×43×18) 2,500/2,962 tD. *Complement:* 260 officers and men.
Armament: Guns: Two 4.5-inch HA/LA. Two 20mm AA. *Missiles:*
Quadruple Seacat (surface to air) launcher. *A/S Weapons:* One Limbo
3-barrelled depth charge mortar. Wasp helicopter with homing torpedoes.
Propulsion: Twin screws driven by double-reduction-geared steam turbines:
30,000 shp: 30 knots. Of the 26 'Leander' Class ships, the last ten were built
with a beam broader by 2 feet. Like the earlier ships they are being rearmed
with modern weaponry.

217
SCYLLA Frigate 'Broad Beamed Leander' Class. *Completed:* 1970.
Description and details as for DIOMEDE (Plate 216). The ship is seen here
leaving Portsmouth Harbour for the Review Anchorage.

218
ROTHESAY Frigate Modified Type 12 'Rothesay' Class. *Completed:*
1960 (370×41×17¼) 2,380/2,800 tD. *Complement:* 235 officers and men.
Armament: Guns: Two 4.5-inch HA/LA. Two 20mm AA. *Missiles:* One
quadruple launcher for Seacat (surface to air) *A/S Weapons:* One Limbo
3-barrelled depth charge mortar. One Wasp helicopter. *Propulsion:* Twin
screws driven by double-reduction-steam turbines: 30,000 shp: 30 knots.
These ships are a development of the 'Whitby' Class (qv) but have improved
layout. All nine were modernised and refitted during 1966-72, and each was
then given an A/S helicopter and Seacat missiles. They are essentially A/S
frigates. The ship is seen here leaving Portsmouth Harbour for the Review
Anchorage.

219

220

221

219
BRIGHTON Frigate Modified Type 12 'Rothesay' Class. *Completed:*
1961. Description and details as for ROTHESAY (Plate 218) This view of
the ship shows the helicopter hangar with the Seacat launcher mounted on top.
The Limbo mortar can be seen at the forward end of the quarterdeck.

220
BERWICK Frigate Modified Type 12 'Rothesay' Class. *Completed:*
1961   Description and details as for ROTHESAY (Plate 218).

221
EASTBOURNE Frigate Type 12 'Whitby' Class. *Completed:* 1958
(369¾×41×17) 2,150/2,560 tD. *Complement:* 225 officers and men.
Armaments: None. *Propulsion:* Twin screws driven by double-reduction-
geared steam turbines: 30,430 shp: 31 knots.   Six ships of the class were built.
At the time of the Review only two remained and were active as training ships.
EASTBOURNE was a training ship for engine-room personnel. TORQUAY,
also at the Review, was a Navigation Training and Trials ship. (See also Plate
160). For disposal 1981.

222

223

224

222
GURKHA Frigate Type 81 'Tribal' Class. *Completed:* 1963
(360×42½×17½) 2,300/2,700 tD. *Complement:* 253 officers and men.
Armament: Two 4.5-inch HA/LA guns: two 20mm AA guns. *Missiles:* Two
quadruple Seacat (surface to air) launchers. *A/S Weapons:* Limbo 3-barrelled
mortar. One helicopter. *Propulsion:* COSAG: combined single-reduction-
geared steam turbine: 12,500 shp and booster gas turbine, 7,500 shp: 1 screw:
28 knots. One of a class of seven general purpose frigates built for duties
overseas such as the Persian Gulf. The ships carried the names of famous
'Tribal' Class destroyers of WWII. For disposal 1981.

223
NUBIAN Frigate Type 81 'Tribal' Class — general purpose. *Completed:*
1962. Description and details as for GURKHA. For disposal 1981. (Plate
222).

224
SALISBURY Frigate Type 61 Aircraft-Direction Frigate. *Completed:*
1957 (339¾×40×15½) 2,170/2,408 tD. *Complement:* 237 officers and
men. *Armament: Guns:* Two 4.5-inch HA/LA and two 20mm AA. *Missiles:*
One quadruple Seacat (surface to air) launcher. *A/S Weapons:* One three-
barrelled Squid depth charge launcher. *Propulsion:* Eight diesel motors
geared to two shafts: 14,400 bhp: 24 knots. One of a class of four ships fitted
with advanced radar and other electronic equipment. One of the ships, HMS
LLANDAFF became UMAR FAROOQ of the Bangladesh Navy in 1976.

225

226

227

225

LYNX Frigate Type 41 'Leopard' Class. *Completed:* 1957
(339¾×40×16) 2,300/2,520 tD. *Complement:* 235 officers and men.
Armament: Guns: Four 4.5-inch HA/LA and one 40mm AA. No missile
capability. *A/S Weapons:* One Squid 3-barrelled depth charge mortar.
Propulsion: Eight diesel engines driving twin screws: 14,400 bhp: 24 knots
There were four ships in the class, designed for the AA protection of surface
ships. They were stabilised. At the time of the Review only LYNX and
JAGUAR remained and both were in reserve. The welded hulls and the power
plants of these ships were identical with those of the Type 61 'Salisbury' Class
(qv). For disposal 1981.

226

DUNDAS Frigate (A/S) Type 14. *Completed:* 1956 (310×33×15½)
1,180/1,456 tD. *Complement:* 140 officers and men. *Armament:* Two
40mm Bofors AA guns. *A/S Weapons:* Two Limbo 3-barrelled depth charge
mortars. *Propulsion:* Single-reduction-geared steam turbine driving a single
screw: 15,000 shp: 27¾ knots.   DUNDAS and HARDY (Plate 227) were two
of the last four ships of a class of 12. They were cheaply constructed of
prefabricated sections which later were strengthened to enable the ships to be
used on fishery protection duties. In 1977 the remaining ships of this class were
used for training duties but all were for disposal in 1981.

227

HARDY Frigate (A/S) Type 14. *Completed:* 1955. Description and
details as for DUNDAS (Plate 226) She formed part of the Second Frigate
Squadron at the Review but was used only for training.

228

229

230

228
DREADNOUGHT Nuclear Fleet Submarine. *Completed:* 1963
(265¾×32¼×26) 3,000/4,000 tD. *Complement:* 88 officers and men.
Armament: Six 21-inch torpedo tubes. *Propulsion:* single-reduction-geared
steam turbines receiving steam from a pressurised-water-cooled reactor. Single
screw. 28+ knots dived. This was the first nuclear submarine in the Royal
Navy and is designed specifically as an anti-submarine unit. In 1971 she
travelled submerged to the North Pole and surfaced there on the 3 March after
voyaging for 750 miles under pack ice.

229
CHURCHILL Nuclear Fleet Submarine. *Completed:* 1970
(285×33¼×27) 3,500/4,500 tD. *Complement:* 103 officers and men.
Armament: Six 21-inch torpedo tubes. *Propulsion:* Single screw driven by
single-reduction-geared turbines receiving steam from a pressurised water
cooled nuclear reactor. 28+ knots dived. One of five 'Valiant' Class boats, the
design being a development of that of DREADNOUGHT (Plate 228).

230
SUPERB Nuclear Fleet Submarine. *Completed:* 1976 (272×33¼×27)
3,500/4,500 tD. *Complement:* 97 officers and men. *Armament:* five 21-inch
torpedo tubes. *Propulsion:* Single screw driven by single-reduction-geared
steam turbines receiving steam from pressurised water-cooled reactor.
25+knots/30+knots. In 1977 this was one of the latest attack submarines
of the Royal Navy.

231

232

231
ORACLE Submarine. *Completed:* 1963 295¼×26½×18) 1,610/2,410 tD. *Complement:* 68 officers and men. *Armament:* Eight 21-inch torpedo tubes. *Propulsion:* (surface) Twin screws driven by two 16-cylinder V-type diesel engines totalling 3,680bhp: 12 knots. (Dived) Two dc electric motors of 6,000 shp: 17 knots. In the 'Oberon' Class submarines, part of the bridge structure is fabricated of glass fibre laminate.

232
SEALION Patrol Submarine. *Completed:* 1961 (295¼×26½×18) 1,610/2,410 tD. *Complement:* 71 officers and men. *Armament:* Eight 21-inch torpedo tubes. (Carries 30 torpedoes). Can be used as a mine layer. *Propulsion:* Twin screws driven by two V-type 16-cylinder diesel engines totalling 3,680 bhp for a surface speed of 12 knots. Two dc electric motors of 6,000 shp for a dived speed of 17 knots. 10 boats of this class were at the Review.

233

234

233
OLWEN (ex OLYNTHUS '67) RFA Large Fleet Tanker. *Completed:*
1965 (648×84×34) 10,890 (light)/36,000 tD. (18,604 tG). Air
conditioned. *Complement:* 87 officers and men. *Propulsion:* Two Pametrada
steam turbines double-reduction-geared to single screw shaft: 26,500shp: 19
knots. The ship has a helicopter hangar and landing platform aft with
accommodation for three Wessex helicopters. These can be used to transfer
stores from OLWEN to other ships some distance away. She can replenish
ships with oil by a pipeline trailed astern or by pipes supported by long,
specially designed, derricks with the receiving ship abeam. It is even possible to
replenish two ships, one on each beam, simultaneously. The photograph of
OLWEN arriving at the Review Anchorage, shows clearly the three derricks
with their supported pipes on the starboard side of the ship. There are, of
course, three similar derricks on the port side.

234
PEARLEAF RFA Support Tanker. *Completed:* 1960. (568×71¾×30)
25,790 full load Displacement. (12,363 tG) *Propulsion:* Single screw.
Doxford 6-cylinder diesel engine: 8,800 bhp: 16 knots. This is one of several
chartered support tankers, the owners in this case being Jacobs and Partners,
London. PEARLEAF is equipped to replenish on either beam or astern and
she can carry three different grades of oil. She is seen here arriving at the
Review Anchorage.

235
STROMNESS RFA Stores Support Ship. *Completed:* 1967
(524×72×25½) 9,010 (light) 16,792 tD. (12,369 tG) *Complement:* 105
officers and men. Air conditioned. *Propulsion:* Two 8-cylinder diesel engines
driving a single screw: 11,520 bhp: 18 knots. Helicopter platform aft to
enable stores to be transferred at sea. STROMNESS is one of three sister ships
and is seen approaching her anchorage in the Review lines. Her sister
LYNESS carried official guests in the wake of BRITANNIA

236
WOODLARK (ex YAXHAM) Inshore Survey Ship converted from
Inshore Minesweeper. *Completed:* 1958 (107½×22×5½) 120/160 tD.
Complement: 18 officers and men. *Propulsion:* Diesel engines driving twin
screws: 1,100 bhp: 14 knots. With her sister WATERWITCH she is engaged
in survey duties in inshore waters at home.

237
FOX Coastal Survey Ship 'Bulldog' Class. *Completed:* 1968
(189×37½×12) 800/1,088 tD. *Complement:* 38 officers and men.
Propulsion: Four 8-cylinder 4-cycle diesel engines geared to two shafts with
controllable pitch propellors. 2,000 bhp: 15 knots. This is one of four ships
intended for overseas survey work. They are air-conditioned and have
sophisticated instrumentation to ensure accurate positioning. A 28½ft
surveying motor boat is carried.

235

236

237

238

239

240

238
AGILE One of five 'Confiance' Class tugs *Completed:* 1959
($154\frac{3}{4}\times35\times11$) 760 tons full load displacement. *Complement:* 29 officers
and men. *Armament:* One 40mm AA gun. *Propulsion:* Four diesel motors
geared to two shafts with two controllable pitch propellors: 1,800 bhp:
13 knots. AGILE is operated by the Royal Maritime Auxiliary Service for
ocean towing. Seen here, she was one of the many small ships acting as ferries
between Portsmouth and ships at the Review Anchorage.

239
GRIPER 'Director' Class Tug *Completed:* 1958 ($94\times24\frac{1}{2}\times12$) 710 full
load displacement. *Complement:* 21 officers and men. *Propulsion:* Diesel-
electric: two independently driven paddle wheels: 2,000 bhp: 13 knots. Seen
here, GRIPER was carrying relatives and friends from Portsmouth Harbour
to various ships in the Review Anchorage. Sold in 1980.

240
HARLECH Fleet Tender One of 31 'Cartmel' Class single screw diesel
ships of 320 bhp: $10\frac{1}{2}$ knots. They are of 143 tons full load Displacement, with
a *Complement* of 6. *Dimensions* are $80\times21\times6\frac{1}{2}$ft. HARLECH was kept busy
on ferry duties during the Review.

241

MELBOURNE. (ex MAJESTIC) *Australia* Aircraft Carrier *Completed:* 1955 (70½×80¼×25½ Flight deck width 126) 16,000/19,966 tD. *Complement:* 1,335 officers and men including air personnel. *Armament:* Twelve 40mm AA guns. *Aircraft:* Eight jet fighters, six tracker aircraft; 10 Sea King A/S helicopters. *Propulsion:* Twin screws driven by single-reduction-geared steam turbines: 42,000 shp: 23 knots. The design of the ship was altered and modernised after being laid down in 1943. She was not completed until 12 years later and has an angled flight deck and a steam catapult. She was transferred to the Royal Australian Navy on completion.

242

243

242

BRISBANE *Australia* Destroyer 'Perth' Class. *Completed:* 1967 (Built in USA to design similar to that of the 'Charles F. Adams' Class) (437×47¼×20) 3,370/4,618 tD. *Complement:* 333 officers and men *Armament: Guns:* Two 5-inch HA/LA. *Missiles:* One single launcher for Tartar (surface to air). *A/S Weapons:* Two single launchers for Ikara system (behind the deckhouse between the funnels). Six torpedo tubes for homing torpedoes. *Propulsion:* Twin screws driven by double-reduction-geared steam turbines: 70,000 shp 35 knots. Much of the superstructure is fabricated from aluminium. The ship is air-conditioned.

243

HURON *Canada* Destroyer 'Tribal' Class. *Completed:* 1972 (426×50×14½) 4,200 full load Displacement. *Complement:* 285 officers and men, including 40 air unit. *Armament: Guns:* One 5-inch HA/LA. *Missiles:* Two quadruple launchers for Sea Sparrow (surface to air). *A/S Weapons:* One Mark 10 Limbo. Six torpedo tubes for A/S homing torpedoes. Two Sea King helicopters carrying homing torpedoes. *Propulsion:* COGOG. Two controllable pitch propellers. Two gas turbines as main engines: 50,000 shp: 29+ knots. Two gas turbines totalling 7,400 shp for cruising. This stern view shows her variable depth sonar and one helicopter on the launching platform aft of the hangar.

244

245

244
CANTERBURY *New Zealand* Frigate 'Broad-beamed Leander' Class. *Completed:* 1971 (372×43×18) 1,470/2,990 tD. *Complement:* 243 officers and men. *Armament: Guns:* Two 4.5 HA/LA: two 20mm AA. *Missiles:* One quadruple Seacat (surface to air). *A/S Weapons:* Two torpedo tubes. One Wasp helicopter. *Propulsion:* Twin screws driven by double-reduction-geared steam turbines: 30,000 shp: 28 knots. There are small differences between this New Zealand ship and the British ships of the same class and her maximum speed is given as 2 knots less than that of the RN ships.

245
UDAYGIRI *India* Frigate 'Broad Beamed Leander' Class. *Completed:* 1975 (372×43×18) 2,450/2,800 tD. *Complement:* 263 officers and men. *Armaments: Guns:* Two 4.5-inch HA/LA. Two 40mm AA. *Missiles:* Two Seacat (surface to air) quadruple launchers. *A/S Weapons:* One 3-barrelled Limbo depth charge mortar. *Propulsion:* Twin screws: double-reduction-geared steam turbines: 30,000 shp: 30 knots. One of a class of six ships built in India to the designs of the British Broad-beamed 'Leander' Class. Floodlights for use on the night of the Review can be seen on the ends of small booms in the vertical position. Each boom can be lowered horizontally to allow the lights to illuminate the ship's side.

246

247

246
GODETIA *Belgium* Support Ship. *Completed:* 1966 (301×46×11½)
1,700/2,500 tD. *Complement:* 100 officers and men. *Armament:* Two
40mm AA guns. *Propulsion:* Four MAN diesel engines geared to two shafts
with controllable pitch propellers: 19 knots. There is a landing platform for a
light helicopter.

247
MØEN *Denmark* Minelayer 'Falster' Class. *Completed:* 1964
(252½×41×10) 1,900 full load displacement. *Complement:* 120 officers and
men. *Armament: Guns:* Four 3-inch in twin mountings. *Missiles:*
Seasparrow (surface to air) launchers. *Mines:* Up to 400 can be carried.
Propulsion: Twin screws driven by two geared diesels 4,800 shp: 17 knots.
The hull is strengthened against ice.

248

249

248
DUQUESNE *France* Destroyer. *Completed:* 1970 (517×60×20) 5,090/
6,090 tD. *Complement:* 426 officers and men *Armament: Guns:* One
3.9-inch HA/LA. Two 30mm AA. *Missiles:* One twin Masurca (surface to
air) launcher. Four Exocet (surface to surface) launchers. *A/S Weapons:* One
single Malafon A/S launcher. Four tubes (two each side) for A/S torpedoes.
Propulsion: Twin screws driven by double-reduction-geared steam turbines:
72,500 shp: 34 knots. Four automatically controlled boilers supplying steam at
640 psi and 842°F of superheat. There are two ships of the class, SUFFREN
being the other. They are stabilised and fully air conditioned. They have
variable depth sonar (seen in the photograph) and very sophisticated radar and
other sensors. Surprisingly, neither ship carries a helicopter.

249
HAMBURG *West Germany* Destroyer. *Completed:* 1964. A sister ship
to BAYERN (Plate 173) for description and details.

250

251

252

253

254

250
KAMAN *Iran* Fast Attack Craft — Missile. *Completed:* 1976 (154¼×23¼×6½) 249/275 tD. *Complement:* 30 officers and men. *Armament: Guns:* One 76mm HA/LA. One 40mm AA. *Missiles:* Two twin launchers for Harpoon (surface to surface). *Propulsion:* Four screws driven by four diesel engines. 14,400 bhp: 36 knots. KAMAN and her sister ship ZUBIN attended the Review. She is seen here approaching Portsmouth Harbour. She later left for the Review Anchorage.

251
ARDITO Destroyer *Italy*. *Completed:* 1973 (446½×47×15) 3,600/ 4,400 tD. *Complement:* 380 officers and men. *Armament: Guns:* Two 5-inch HA/LA: four 3-inch AA. *Missiles:* One Tartar surface to air launcher. *A/S Weapons:* Six A/S torpedo tubes. Two Sea King helicopters. *Propulsion:* Twin screws driven by single-reduction-geared steam turbines: 73,000 shp: 33 knots. The second of two ships of distinctly American appearance.

252
TROMP *Netherlands* Destroyer. *Completed:* 1975 (454×48½×15) 4,300/ 5,400 tD. *Complement:* 306 officers and men. *Armament: Guns:* Two 4.7-inch HA/LA in a twin turret forward. *Missiles:* Two quadruple Harpoon (surface to surface) launchers in 'B' gun position. One Tartar (surface to air)

launcher aft. Seasparrow (short range surface to air) system. *A/S Weapons:* ASW torpedoes. One Lynx helicopter. *Propulsion:* COGOG. Twin screws each driven by an Olympus gas turbine geared to the screw shafts: 50,000 shp: 30 knots. Two Tyne gas turbines for cruising: 8,000 shp. TROMP was one of the 'best balanced' ships seen at the Review. She has powerful arguments against surface ships, aircraft and submarines and has very efficient radar and other sensors.

253
NARVIK *Norway* Frigate. 'Oslo' Class. *Completed:* 1966. A sister ship to BERGEN (Plate 183) which see for description and details. Seen above the ship is a fly-past of helicopters at the Review.

254
ALMIRANTE MAGALHAES CORREA *Portugal* Frigate. *Completed:* 1968 (314½×36¾×17½) 1,450/1,914 tD. *Complement:* 166 officers and men. *Armament: Guns:* Four 3-inch. *A/S Weapons:* Six A/S torpedo tubes: two 4-barrelled mortars: two depth charge throwers. *Propulsion:* Single screw powered by double-reduction-geared steam turbines: 20,000 shp: 27 knots. This ship is built to the design of the prefabricated 'Dealey' Class of the United States Navy and modified to meet the needs of the Portuguese Navy.

255

256

255
BERK Frigate *Turkey. Completed:* 1972 (311¾×38¾×18)
1,450/1,950 tD. *Complement:* not known. *Armament:* Four 3-inch guns.
A/S Weapons: Six A/S torpedo tubes. One helicopter. *Propulsion:* Four Fiat
diesel engines geared to two shafts: 24,000 shp: 25 knots. There are two ships
in the class and they are the first major warships to be Turkish built. Details of
them are meagre.

256
CALIFORNIA. *USA* Nuclear powered Guided Missile Cruiser.
Completed: 1974 (596×61×31½) 10,150 full load displacement.
Complement: 540 officers and men. *Armament: Guns:* Two 5-inch HA/LA.
Missiles: Two single Tartar (surface to air) launchers, one forward and one
aft. *A/S Weapons:* Four A/S torpedo tubes. One ASROC (ship launched
A/S weapon) 8-tube launcher. *Propulsion:* Twin screws driven by single-
reduction-geared steam turbines supplied with steam from two pressurised-
water-cooled reactors. 30+ knots. One of the two highly sophisticated
cruisers of great power but without helicopter hangars though a landing pad is
provided.

257
BRITANNIA Royal Yacht For description and details see Plate 159.
BRITANNIA is here seen at the head of the lines at the Review Anchorage
with HM the Queen and the Royal Family embarked but before leaving to
review the Fleet at 1430 hours on Tuesday 28 June.

257

258
The helicopter cruiser, HMS TIGER and ships at the *Review*, 1977.

Index